The
Gameshooter's
Pocket Guide

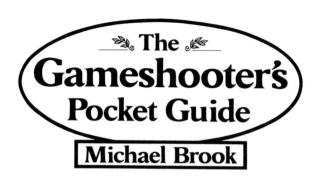

The Gameshooter's Pocket Guide

Michael Brook

Line drawings by Mark Conroy

B. T. Batsford Ltd. London

For Toby
May he enjoy his shooting and others enjoy his company

First published 1990
© Michael Brook

ISBN 0 7134 6580 8

Typeset by Deltatype Ltd, Ellesmere Port
and printed and bound in Great Britain
Courier International, Tiptree, Essex
for the publishers B. T. Batsford Ltd
4 Fitzhardinge Street, London W1H 0AH

CONTENTS

ACKNOWLEDGEMENTS

With any work of this nature, it is inevitable that the author consults, cajoles and tests the good nature of a great many people. This book is no exception, and it is my sincere hope that I have not forgotten anybody; if I have, I apologise and offer my gratitude for their help.

I owe the following a particular debt: For reading the script and contributing helpful suggestions: Jonathan Ruffer, author of *The Edwardian Big Shots*; Mark Colacicchi, friend and shooting companion for many years; John Halford, the Game Conservancy's Regional Secretary for Hampshire; Carl Jeanes, friend and countryman; Nigel Brown, Secretary of the Gun Trade Association; Mark Conroy, artist, ornithologist, fisherman, game shot and General Practitioner when his hobbies permit; George Pelly, who asks little of his shooting but gains so much from it; and Nix Farquharson, my father-in-law, who must have known the text off by heart by the final draft. For technical advice, I am indebted to: Messrs George Wallace, Colin Blanchard and Brian Hughes of BASC; Audrey Wickington of The Home Office; and Nick Mason, shooting agent. For unlimited help with the typescript: Ann Mitchell, Adell Pretty, Stephanie Bates and Jean Browning.

Finally, I owe a considerable debt to Wilson Stephens, Consultant Editor to The Field, and author, for his sage advice and inspiration. This book would not have been published without his unselfish assistance and encouragement.

INTRODUCTION

The inspiration for this book came from the fact that I was an involuntary target twice on formal shoots in the same season. Such experience tends to affect one's enjoyment and, having seen other dangerous incidents in recent years, I felt there was a need for a book about shooting safety and etiquette.

The purposes of this book are twofold. First, to provide an *aide-mémoire* for an experienced shot training a child; typically, a father teaching his son. Secondly, it is aimed at the adult, complete novice who receives an invitation to shoot or who suddenly decides to take up gameshooting.

The child is fortunate in that he can take his time and only be allowed to shoot game once a third party (usually his father) decides he is safe and ready to do so.

It is the adult who is less fortunate and who is most likely to prove a menace to his fellows. He has to absorb a great deal of advice and theory in a very short period; theory that can only be put into context, inevitably, in the shooting field.

Shooting, like any hobby or pursuit, should be a pleasure and should never be at the expense of somebody else's well-being. While this book is about safety, it is also about good manners – in an ideal world, they are one and the same thing. Since we are all fallible, not least the author, it is no bad thing to revise a few sound principles occasionally; it is a very rare person who can put his hand on his heart and swear that he has never fired a potentially dangerous shot – I know I cannot.

It has not been my intention to describe every possible type of shoot. Thus, in Chapter One, I describe an average, informal, driven shoot, which although privately owned would be similar if syndicated. I believe that this approach will cater for the great majority of people new to gameshooting. Although the views and opinions expressed in this book are one man's, and based to a great extent on his experience, they are also bolstered by reference to other sources considerably wiser, more knowledgeable and experienced than the author.

There is increasing political and media pressure on gameshooting which has led to the drawing up of a Code of Good

Game Shooting Practice by a joint committee formed by the BASC, BFSS and The Game Conservancy. Every element of this code is included in the relevant parts of this book.

Misbehaviour, due to ignorance, uncertainty, or bad manners in a small minority, can bring the whole sport into disrepute and potentially ruin it for the majority. If this small book reduces the risk of that happening, then it will have achieved its purpose.

1
A DAY'S SHOOTING

This chapter cannot be foolproof – for those with natural good manners it may be a useful memory-jogger but it is not a failsafe for those with limited consideration for others. Suffice it to say that rudeness is most unlikely to result in a second invitation to shoot for a guest who has sinned.

'Sorry' is one word which should always be ready to hand – it costs nothing and can turn a potential disaster into a success, sometimes, that is. Successive poaching of a neighbouring Gun's birds, followed by a shrill 'Sorry!' becomes a totally threadbare excuse after only two uses' though.

It is remarkable, too, how reassuring an apology can be, particularly if a neighbouring Gun has shot a bit too close to oneself for comfort. This sort of apology takes some courage to admit but is much appreciated.

The first maxim must be: 'Be safe at all times', followed by: 'If in doubt, ask.'

What follows is what might happen on a day's shooting although the occasion when one might shoot grouse, duck and pheasant on the same shoot on the same day are fairly rare. While such a day might be possible in Scotland or the North of England, because of the presence of grouse, it is not exactly typical and has been contrived to make various points. Grouse will most certainly not be found on shoots in Hampshire or Sussex, for example, however grand the shoot!

Preliminaries

'George, its Charles Chute-Strait. I was wondering whether you could shoot at Feudal Park on the fifteenth? You can? Oh, excellent. Look, old chap, it's very informal . . .' George knew Charles too well and realised that 'informal' did not mean jeans and an old combat jacket. ' . . . We meet at the house at 0915 hours. We'll have a go at grouse and pheasants so bring plenty of cartridges. Oh, yes, and do stay for the evening flight.' George did a quick mental check list: Charles had told him where to go and when, what to wear and a rough idea of what to

6

expect; what else? 'Ah, Charles. Do you mind if I bring the dog or would you prefer me to leave him behind?'

'No, delighted as long as he's well-behaved. I'm sure you'd keep him tethered anyway if he wasn't too steady. No, as I say, delighted.'

'One last question, Charles. Shall I bring lunch?'[1]

'Good point, old chap, I should have mentioned it. Please bring your own. We gather in the old lodge for lunch, so it'll be fairly dry and comfortable. Anyway, we'll look forward to seeing you on the fifteenth. Be good, you old rogue. Byee.'

George was aware that Charles had not mentioned Fiona, his wife. He would miss her company, but decided that additional guests must obviously not be expected. At least he'd have Tom, his Labrador, who was always a perfect companion.

'Why's he called Tom?' he was often asked, to which his pat reply was: 'Because it's an easy name to bellow and his brothers were called Dick and Harry.'

Note (1) This is the stage at which you can get all your questions answered. It is rash and impolite to turn up with, for example, a companion without first clearing it with your host. If you receive a written invitation as opposed to a verbal one, it is imperative that you reply to it without delay.

Arrival

George arrived at Feudal Park at 0900 hours, in good time to put on his boots, jacket and other gear and to assemble his gun and equipment. His father had always said: 'Early to shoot, late to dinner, me boy; i.e. get to the shoot in good time or you might ruin your host's plans.'[2]

Although he had put out everything the night before, prior to setting off he had meticulously re-checked his kit, just in case he had missed something. Although he had not done so personally, he knew people who had left their guns behind and he too had forgotten the odd item which tended, however trivial, to

7

overshadow an otherwise good day. The worst thing he had done in the past was to forget his waxed cotton jacket, which was very inconvenient since it contained several necessities.

Thus he quickly ran through the list: Waxed Cotton Jacket, Money for tips and petrol on the way home, Cap, Gloves, Scarf, Leggings, First Aid Kit, Pencil and paper, Hip-flask, Cartridge bag (full), Cartridge belt (full), Gun, Gunsleeve, Boots and Socks, Dog, Dog whistle, Dog lead, Dog's waterbowl, Dog's water and a few biscuits. What else? Ah, yes, Dog's towelling bag (so much better than just a towel) and Earplugs. Torch for the duckflight, plus Lunch and Liquid refreshment, of course.

He was not the first to arrive and quickly introduced himself to those who had arrived before him; he noticed too that another Gun had brought a guest and was assiduously introducing him to everybody[3]. Another gun had brought his son, who was not going to shoot but shadow his father as part of his tutoring in the mores of shooting. He was careful to keep Tom on the lead but gave him the chance to accustom himself to the scenery and do what most dogs like to do after a journey.

Notes: (2) Late arrival could ruin a carefully planned day and also result in extra expense for the host or syndicate.

(3) Do not be shy so that people can get to know you quickly. Also, if you are an established member of a shoot, make strangers welcome.

The Briefing

At 0915, Charles Chute-Strait gathered the Guns together and introduced the guests[4]. Then he outlined the day ahead before getting the Guns to draw for pegs. 'We number from the right and move up two places each drive.'

George listened very attentively to his host, even though he was keen to chat to one of the other Guns, who was an old friend he had not seen for a while. Thus, significantly, he discovered that they would not be coming back to the cars before the end of the day. This meant taking cartridge bags and lunch on the trailer. He had forgotten lunch one day and shivered with embarrassment as he recalled the humiliation he had felt at accepting his fellow Guns' charity; actually he had done rather well, but preferred not to have to repeat the experience.

As Charles finished his briefing, George went up to him and said quietly, 'Charles, what's the Keeper's name and what can we shoot?'

'Jem Morgan's his name. Good of you to ask. Shoot pheasants, partridges, grouse. Don't shoot hares since they're a bit scarce in these parts at the moment. Oh, and please don't shoot foxes,' Charles replied nonchalantly, secretly kicking himself for not having included such a fundamental point in his briefing[5].

George made a point, before climbing on the trailer, of introducing himself to the Keeper.

The trailer was somewhat draughty, but just one variation on the transport theme, George reflected as they bumped up a rutted track to the first drive. Sometimes, on a shoot, there was no need for transport at all, sometimes Guns were moved in Landrovers and other four-wheel drive vehicles (very smart) and sometimes they took their cars from drive to drive. It all depended on distances to be covered.

Notes: (4) The number of guns may vary between six and twelve, eight being an average figure. Too many guns are difficult to control and to fit comfortably around coverts, when the usual distance between guns is about 40 yards.

(5) Most shoots have an agreement with their local hunt and, therefore, do not shoot foxes. Foxes tend to be shot only where the hunt cannot safely go. Even then, unless a fox is within a few feet, it should be left, since foxes are hard to kill with a shotgun and can easily be only wounded.

The First Drive

They arrived at the start of the first drive, which, due to the lie of the land, George judged to be a pheasant drive. Charles escorted George to his peg which was marked by a stick with a split in the top and a number inserted in the split. 'The birds will come from that direction. Just watch out for the walking Gun who will appear to your left late on,' said Charles helpfully in a low voice before wandering off to his peg.

On the way, Charles nudged one of the guns who was strolling towards his peg and talking loudly to another gun, indicating with a finger to his lips to keep quiet[6]. George took his bearings and ensured that the guns either side of him acknowledged where he was. He surveyed all the ground around him in a 360–degree arc so that he knew instinctively the danger spots, where not to shoot, where the birds might fly to, and that there were no people who should not be there[7]. Having tethered Tom, he took his gun from its sleeve, checked the barrels were clear[8], loaded it, checked the safety catch was on, and stood with the gun held under his arm pointing at the ground, waiting for the pheasants.

Nothing happened for ages but he resisted the temptation to talk to his fellow Guns and refrained too from fiddling with his gun.

Suddenly a voice cried, 'Over!'[9] He looked ahead and saw a hen pheasant flying towards him. He started to raise his gun but, because in his estimation the bird was too low, did not fire at it. The hen was followed soon afterwards by a cock which was nearer him than the Gun on his right. He was just raising his gun when there was a bang and the bird fell dead behind him. 'Sorry, I think that should really have been yours,' said the perpetrator, almost too hastily. The same Gun then shot at a bird which was patently out of range. Unfortunately he pricked it and it flew on quite strongly, even though obviously wounded. Tom looked up at George as if to say, 'You wouldn't dream of doing such a thing, would you, Master?'

Before he could dwell on his neighbour's misdemeanours any

further, he was faced with a steady stream of birds. Carefully selecting one bird at a time, rather than flitting from target to target before firing, he shot several birds before a lull occurred. Tom looked at him admiringly, wagging his tail happily and obviously proud of Master's prowess; George resisted the temptation to let Tom off to start picking the dead birds, although his neighbour's dog was running loose, picking other Guns' birds. Tom was not impressed either[10].

As the beaters hove in sight, George raised his barrels skywards to show that he had seen them and would only take high birds or birds behind. Jem Morgan blew a whistle as a signal that the drive was over and Guns should unload. George turned his barrels away from the beaters and unloaded, keeping his gun under his arm but open, before releasing Tom to retrieve his birds.

Although he enjoyed carrying his birds to the game cart – as a manifestation of his success – he cheerfully handed over his birds to a beater who offered to carry them[11].

As he and Tom walked back to the trailer, they were joined by a rather tiresome individual. 'I got six that time for sixteen cartridges. I reckon that makes my average for the season about two point seven cartridges per bird.' George smiled politely at him and said something vague like, 'Really? Well done. I never dare tally up because I'm sure it would be too much of a shock.' Somehow it seemed *infra dig* to work out one's cartridge–to–kill ratio, and talking about it was tantamount to boasting. Besides, he never had any real idea how many cartridges he had fired and, if he did, it would probably make him give up shooting altogether.

George was about to climb aboard the trailer when Charles said, 'George, old chap, would you like to walk with the beaters this drive? It's usually good value . . . quite busy.' George duly joined the beaters and was gratified when Jem Morgan said, 'You're in the hot seat this time sir, the royal box so to speak. By the way, it's a special day today since, because of the drives we're doing, you could theoretically shoot at least eight different

11

species. Leastways, the record's eight, won by Mr Chute-Strait's father in 1952.'

It sounded a bit like a challenge but, before George could query it, the Keeper had turned away to direct his beaters.

Notes: (6) Game is easily disturbed and, if forewarned, will sit tight, thereby ruining that drive and sport for everybody else. Inevitably this also means that people's money is being wasted; therefore, noise and talking should be avoided as much as possible.

(7) There may well be pickers-up. Normally they should be well back, concealed and out of range but beware, since some tend to creep towards the Guns without you or themselves realizing it.

(8) The slightest blockage could cause a burst barrel when fired.

(9) It is hard to dictate when to warn a neighbour of approaching quarry and it should only be done if he is going to be genuinely taken by surprise, otherwise it can be most off-putting. It is wise to bide your time and see if regular members do it.

(10) Dogs should be kept in until the end of a drive and never released before. Loose dogs can be shot mistakenly, can easily disturb the game from both the present and subsequent drives, and upset other Guns.

(11) It is customary to let beaters carry the bag unless they are overburdened and would appreciate help – do not force the issue.

The Second Drive

George was in the centre of the beating line. He kept Tom to heel rather than letting him work out front. Had he not been shooting, and therefore able to devote more attention to his dog, he would have let him do so, having first ascertained it was all right to do so from the Keeper. Perhaps, if another chance to walk occurred later in the day, he would let Tom work out in front; by that stage he should have worked off his exuberance and be steady and reliable. He was worried lest the dog go too far out and out of immediate control. He had seen several dogs ruined in this way; not every dog can adjust, on alternate drives, from straight retriever to working dog, quartering the ground, and back to retriever again. Working in front is great fun for a dog and hard work, but there are many potential diversions which may cause the dog to disgrace itself (and its master) by ignoring its master's instructions in its excitement.

George thoroughly enjoyed walking, especially since, on a cold day, it offered the chance to warm up. Also, because he knew nobody would be behind him, he could shoot with almost complete confidence that he was unlikely to shoot someone he did not know was there. As the beaters began their advance through the covert, George hung back slightly.

Almost immediately, a hare ran in front and then behind him, whereupon he took aim and was about to pull the trigger when he remembered his host's exhortation to spare hares. Nevertheless, he shot the rabbit which darted out from under a tree stump shortly after. Tom retrieved it and, after squeezing its abdomen to drain its bladder, George put it in the game pocket of his jacket[12].

As the drive continued, George spoke to the beaters either side of him which they appreciated since, as often as not, Guns never spoke to them from one drive to the next. Whether it was coincidence or not, they subsequently seemed to flush a lot of birds which flew in his direction. Fortunately the beaters and Tom picked his kills because, after a while, he could not mark their whereabouts accurately.

He was walking along, contemplating the satisfaction of taking part in such a good day, when one of the beaters yelled, 'cock back.'[13] Instinctively he looked up, saw a woodcock jinking through the trees, raised his gun and, as he was about to fire, saw a second woodcock. He fired at the first, saw it drop

13

and then swung onto the second. It too dropped dead in a bush behind him. Tom marked the birds but, like many dogs, displayed a manifest distaste for retrieving woodcock. Nevertheless, between George and a beater they picked both birds.

'By, that was good shooting. A right and a left at woodcock is worthy of a knighthood,' said a beater who turned out to be a local doctor, who often came along for the exercise and enjoyment of seeing others doing something well, even though he was not a shooting man. 'I'll be your witness if you like so that you can claim your bottle of whisky from the Shooting Times.' George had heard that the Shooting Times offered such a prize but had never met anyone who had won it.

He did not shoot anything else that drive and would have been content to have finished the day then, even though he realized that there were probably two more drives at least before lunch. He had had great sport already, Tom had performed immaculately, and it seemed to be tempting fate to go on.

Notes: (12) For safety reasons, ground game should be left except if walking. They should be shot to your rear and then only if you are absolutely certain there is nobody behind.

(13) Woodcock are frequently identified by beaters by the cry 'cock'. On cock–pheasant–only days, beaters may help the guns by calling 'Hen' or 'Cock'.

The Third Drive

'Dead-eye; eh, George?' said Charles as they met by the trailer again. 'The beaters are positively buzzing about your skill. They say you're incapable of missing. That's good, because you're in a good spot this next drive.'

George suddenly wondered whether such faith and implied responsibility might be over-generosity on Charles' part; somehow, he had an intuition that he might not manage to live up to this heady reputation for much longer. He was a reasonable shot but inconsistent, like the majority of people are, and experienced enough to acknowledge his weaknesses and to recognize the warning signals when he might lose form. Just now, the signals were beginning to flash at him with depressing familiarity.

When the trailer halted, the Guns began to dismount. One of the Guns, instead of handing his gun to someone while he climbed down, kept the gun in his hand. As he jumped down, he hit the barrels with a loud thud against the tailgate. Without bothering to check his gun he strode off to his peg.

George went to his peg, speculating about the severity of the damage to the gun and surprised at the owner's seeming indifference. He was just loading his gun when a pheasant got up in front of the Gun on his left. The bird could not have been more than ten feet from the end of the barrels. There was a great cloud of feathers as if a duvet had been assassinated, and the bird seemed to explode, mutilated beyond recognition. 'What a dreadful waste,' mused George to himself, hardly bothering to listen to the perpetrator's blustering excuse: 'Good Lord, did you see that? My shot must have balled.'

George had heard of shot balling, a phenomenon where the shot fused to form an almost solid ball. This is liable to destroy a bird if it makes contact, but not pluck it, as happens when the bird takes the full force of the standard contents of a cartridge. It is a very rare occurrence indeed. George also knew when a bird had been shot at absurdly close range.

Four cocks flew over as the man was reloading, between him and George. George fired at one, which he knew he had hit. Almost simultaneously, there was a shot from his left followed by: 'My bird I think, old man.' George's first reaction was to argue the toss since he was absolutely certain that it was his bird but held his tongue after a moment's hesitation, thinking that a true sportsman would not be so greedily eager to claim the spoils.

It was pointless to argue over something so trivial, even if it happened more than once. More importantly it would have been rude to his host to disrupt the harmony of the day; after all, he knew that the bird had fallen to his gun and that was all that mattered. The Gun on his right, afterwards, whispered knowingly in his ear: 'I reckon that was your bird without a shadow of a doubt. I liked the way you didn't fuss over it.'

George's next bird fell dead almost at Tom's feet. As he was reloading, there was a streak of yellow which disappeared even quicker than it had appeared. A yellow Labrador from down the line had stolen the bird from right under Tom's nose before he could make any protest whatsoever. When the thief reached its master he received a congratulatory pat on the head, instead of the remonstration he should have received. George was not surprised, later, that the owner made no effort to apologize for the dog's appalling behaviour. To compound his crime, the yellow Lab had eaten the bird at the peg, failing to mark any of his master's own birds as a result.

George was more concerned about the standard of his own marksmanship which, as he had suspected, was far from satisfactory all of a sudden. He missed pheasant after pheasant to the extent that Tom, instead of sitting up alert, lay down and tried to sleep. Up until this moment, George had ignored all the pigeon he had seen – partly because he felt that to shoot a pigeon early in a drive might disturb the pheasants but mainly because experience from rough shooting had ingrained in him the belief that a shot at pigeon almost inevitably scared off the game.

Pigeon are pests but offer extremely tricky, sporting shooting. It takes quite a few to make a decent meal. Thus, before shooting at them, particularly on a formal shoot, it is sensible to decide whether it is worth it. The best thing to do is to ascertain from one's host whether to take pigeon or not. If you do shoot at a pigeon, you can virtually guarantee that some pheasants will fly over you in perfect formation before you have time to reload.

Anyway, more out of frustration born from desperation, George took a casual shot at a couple of very high pigeons. Hitting one, he fired at the other and was amazed when they both fell to earth quite dead. Tom sat up, looked at the birds and then at George with a look that seemed to say: 'What on earth are you up to?'

Master and dog were disturbed from further telepathic views on pigeon by a great flurry of pheasants which broke cover simultaneously, well out of range and closely followed by a large retriever. The dog had broken loose, charged through the covert and driven the bulk of the birds in the covert towards the Guns in one mass. As usually happens in such instances, the birds were not even flushed anywhere near the Guns. It was an object lesson as to why dogs should be kept under control, how to ruin a drive, and how to incur the host's displeasure. Such actions are unlikely to result in further invitations.

The drive was virtually over, with the beaters still in cover but obviously very close, when a hen broke cover and flew towards the Gun on George's left. The bird seemed to fly straight at the Gun at about head height. The Gun shot at the bird, missing spectacularly but sending his shot straight into the bushes to his front.

Immediately, there was a cry from behind the bush, more indignant than anything else, 'Heh, that hit me.' As it transpired, fortunately, the beater had been peppered but no shots had penetrated his clothing or skin. The Gun whose fault it was, was profoundly apologetic. He was well-versed in shooting etiquette and, to save Charles the embarrassment of sending him home, went up to his host.

'Charles, I am most terribly sorry. Thank God the beater seems to be unscathed . . . I am insured though, if need be, but I don't think it'll be necessary. I will take my leave and go home. Thank you for your kind invitation and for such splendid sport. I just pray that I have not completely ruined the day for you.' With that he departed, despite Charles' protestations that no damage had been done and that he should stay[14].

This incident had a salutary effect on everybody else because the Gun was a very experienced shot. 'Just goes to show,' said another Gun finally, 'that it's those of us who think

17

we're ultra-safe, by virtue of age and experience, who are possibly the most dangerous. It certainly proves we're all human . . .'

Notes: (14) This is a very tricky situation to which there is no easy answer. It is unlikely that the culprit will repeat the error but, whether a guest or member of a syndicate, he should offer to leave, thereby giving his host or captain the choice. The host must be clear and, if the Gun is a guest, either agree to his leaving or insist that he stays. If the shoot is syndicated and the culprit is a member of the syndicate, the captain must make it clear whether the culprit should stay away forevermore or may return the next time. Certainly there would be no question of continuing with that syndicate if he made the same mistake twice.

The culprit must make due apologies to his host and victim. If the victim requires medical treatment, the culprit should avoid admitting liability and should seek legal advice as soon as possible.

The Fourth Drive[15]

Silence descended while the Guns were driven a couple of miles in the trailer to the grouse butts up on the moor which formed a large proportion of the estate. The silence was no bad thing, since grouse are very easy to disturb unless great caution is exercised. George made his way through the heather to his butt, which was nearly on a flank, with one Gun only on his right. He took stock of his situation.

The butt was built from peat turves on top of stone and provided reasonable shelter from the wind. George settled Tom in the butt so that he was completely concealed from view to the front. Then he worked out his arcs and marked them with a couple of empty cartridge cases he found in the bottom of the butt. The idea of this was to give him a firm indication when to swing no further to left or right and, therefore, when to shoot behind. To swing through and beyond the arcs is called 'swinging through the line' and is extremely dangerous since it means that, at some point, a neighbouring Gun will have a loaded gun pointing at him. George was relieved to notice that his neighbours were doing likewise.

Having placed several cartridges to hand on the top of the butt to speed up reloading, he placed his gun conveniently on the top of the butt, so that all he had to do was raise it to his shoulder when the time came. He stood still but, at the same time, continually swept his front with his eyes. He was prepared for a long wait.

The Gun to his left was crouched down below the top of his butt, so that only his eyes and above showed over the top of the butt. To further reduce his silhouette, the Gun kept his barrels below the top of the butt as well. George used to do the same until a canny old keeper told him that grouse are far more likely to be deterred by the sudden appearance of a Gun popping up suddenly from his butt than by somebody in good view but not moving.

George was relieved to discover that his desultory performance in the last drive was only short-lived. He shot five-and-a-half brace of grouse. Several of the birds were shot behind the butt since, once the beaters had appeared, even though technically still well out of range, George wanted to avoid the slightest risk of wounding one. Unlike the Guns, the beaters stood out well due to the safety flashes they wore. Long before they came into sight, their flags, which they waved to make the grouse fly away from them, gave them away by the distinct, sharp, flapping noise they made.

At the end of the drive Tom picked all the birds and it was time to drive down to the lodge for lunch.

Notes: (15) This section describes only a driven grouse shoot. Another, more informal method involves walking-up grouse. Here, Guns walk steadily, taking care for safety's sake to walk straight line abreast, across a moor, flushing grouse as they go.

Guns should not talk except to relay instructions. It can be hard work and calls for alertness and fitness; not a little skill is required in deciding what to carry by avoiding carrying too much clobber (clothing, ammunition and other impedimenta). Birds can usually be taken to front and behind. Dogs should be kept in to avoid flushing birds out of range, and be used to retrieve downed birds.

A similar method is to shoot over Pointers. Here again, Guns walk up but with several Pointers quartering the ground well out to the front. The Pointers are supposed to stop and point as soon as they scent a bird. They remain absolutely motionless until the Guns get in range, whereupon they (or the noise of the Guns moving through the heather) will flush the quarry.

Lunch

Charles Chute-Strait tended to view lunch as a bit of a nuisance; though he enjoyed his food, he enjoyed shooting even more. Nevertheless, he realised the necessity of giving the beaters a rest. Another reason he did not like shooting lunches was because he always reckoned people drank too much, therefore relaxed too much and became distinctly more casual and dangerous as a result.

This might sound cynical and over-generalised but, over the years, his experience had inexorably led him to this conclusion. Statistics proved that the majority of accidents in the shooting field happened after lunch and this automatically reinforced his opinions.

George was of a similar opinion and opted for simple lunches. He either had an all-in stew for cold days followed by some fresh fruit and chocolate or some soup, buns and scotch eggs on milder days. He also took a few biscuits for the dog and some water since, so often, there were never enough puddles to slake a dog's thirst.

To drink, he took some ginger beer, a can or two of beer, sometimes some sherry and sometimes some claret. Rather than drinking much himself, he enjoyed distributing hospitality and found it was a good way to affect a rapport with Guns he might not have got to know in the morning. Nine times out of ten, he found that he took home most of the drink he had brought since people were wary nowadays of being stopped by the police as they drove home[16].

Notes: (16) Guns and cars are equally dangerous in the wrong hands. Some shooting people inevitably drink too much at lunch, confident that they will not be breathalysed while in charge of a gun, and misguidedly thinking that the effects of drink will have worn off before they drive home. In the interim they will be handling a gun, though. Drink in moderation is fine and beneficial in several ways, just as long as it is does not ruin somebody else's pleasure.

The Fifth Drive

With lunch over quite quickly, Charles was about to direct the guns to the trailer but waited when he noticed two of the Guns in their respective cars, talking on their car telephones. Inherent good manners prevented him from displaying the impatience and irritation he felt at this unwarranted delay[17]. Meanwhile the other Guns stood and chatted idly, their guns open and crooked under their arms[18].

Eventually, after several minutes, both missing Guns emerged from their cars and rejoined their fellows, neither offering more than a token apology, both seemingly unaware they had done anything untoward. The Guns climbed on to the trailer to be taken up to the Bog as it was known. This, as the name implied, was a marshy piece of low-lying moor, adjoining the grouse moor. It held an abundance of snipe and, frequently, a few duck.

The Bog was surrounded by an old sheep fence, topped with barbed wire. This was an awkward obstacle. George turned to a man beside him and asked him if he would be good enough to hold his gun while he put Tom and himself over the fence.

Before passing the gun, he opened it to show it was unloaded and closed it again. To assist Tom, he placed his arm along the top strand so that the dog could use it as a step and not risk hurting himself on the barbs. Another Gun removed his jacket and laid it along the top strand of the fence so that his dog could jump over safely. Unfortunately the ground was too soft to give a firm launching point so George, in the end, had to lift Tom bodily over the obstacle. Some years previously, George had lost a dog that had ripped its belly open on wire which was why he tended to be so pedantic about fences these days. Once all the Guns and beaters were over the fence, they lined up in one long line and advanced through the bog. It was tricky going and required one eye firmly fixed on the going and the other peeled for quarry. Everybody stepped from tussock to tussock with much circumspection.

One gun mistook a tussock for terra firma and found himself stepping into icy liquid up to his chest, further downward movement being arrested by his gun wedging across the top of the gap. Laboriously he extracted himself, drained his boots and carefully checked his gun for damage and blocked barrels before continuing.

Two snipe got up in front of George, about five yards apart. Both jinked in that elusive manner unique to snipe before moving low and out of range. George fired both barrels but missed. Snipe are arguably the most difficult birds to shoot, demanding lightning reactions from the Guns. To compound the problem, they are often hard to find once shot, especially because most dogs refuse to pick them.

Some mallard were rash enough, just then, to fly over. George aimed at one and fired. As it was falling, he fired at another and hit it conclusively also. Tom retrieved both subsequently, to his satisfaction.

This drive did not last long but netted fourteen snipe, George managing to account for one in the end, and three mallard.

Notes: (17) While it is sad that business cannot always be separated from pleasure, it must never be allowed to interfere in such a situation; if it does, further invitations to shoot will not be forthcoming. If necessary, business should be conducted during lunch. It is not unknown for people to carry their telephones with them into the shooting field; it is one of the hallmarks of the age; although, even in the Twenties, a few shoot owners apparently installed telephones in their butts. Telephone users should take care never to use their telephones in the middle of drives and to wait to use them quietly between drives, but not delay the start of the next drive; to ensure that they cannot be telephoned so that there is no risk of being called half-way through a drive; and to follow the simple principle that, if the telephone is likely to be intrusive or to disturb the other Guns, it should not be used.

(18) These days, it is customary when not at one's peg to keep one's gun broken (open) and crooked under the arm, with no cartridges in the chambers and with the barrels pointing to the ground. This removes any possible doubt that a gun might be loaded. Only if it is pouring with rain is it acceptable to close the gun. A gunsleeve obviates the problem altogether and is highly recommended for this reason and, as stated elsewhere, to protect the gun.

The Sixth Drive

The sixth drive was marred by a fairly dramatic incident. On the way to the drive one of the Guns (not the same one as mentioned earlier) had knocked his barrels hard against a wall. Carelessly, he omitted to check for any damage. Had he done so he would have seen a serious dent in the left-hand barrel.

He fired at several birds without incident because, each time, he only used one barrel. The problem occurred when he shot at a rabbit which he had no right to shoot at anyway since it was to his front and therefore between the Guns and the beaters. He missed with the first barrel and then fired immediately with the second.

The rabbit was hit but, simultaneously, the left-hand barrel split, miraculously causing no injury to the firer. Little more was said by anybody since the proof of failing to keep a weather eye on safety matters was all too plain to see.

George was in a good stand and fortunately had redis-covered his form. The Guns were lined up in a valley, facing a wood high up on the side of the valley. This resulted in some very high and testing birds, which flew over the Guns before setting their wings and gliding into the cover behind the line on the other side of the valley.

Although George shot twelve pheasants there was little for Tom to do at the end of the drive since a picker-up had picked most of his birds. George was mildly annoyed by the fact there had been a picker-up there in the first place, since he reckoned the picker-up should have been much further back and out of sight. He noticed the picker-up was behind him when, out of pure habit, he had checked at the start of the drive that there was nobody behind. He did this because some years before he had nearly shot a picker-up who had appeared behind him without any warning as he was about to shoot a hare.

The Seventh Drive

The seventh and last drive saw George as a walking Gun again. This time he let Tom work off the lead, having first sought the Keeper's permission.

As they walked up, George kept giving Tom verbal encouragement with the aims of maintaining remote control over the dog, letting his neighbouring beaters know his whereabouts, and to put up any game along his route.

Having been relatively restrained most of the day, Tom was greatly relieved to be doing something interesting and, to him, incredibly exciting. Before long he was working twenty yards out, and then thirty, and then further still. Knowing the implica-tions of letting a dog get too far out, George called his dog to heel only to have him ignore him completely.

Not surprisingly, George was upset. As soon as Tom came within arm's reach he called him to heel, grabbed him by the ruff (he always took off his collar lest he get caught and, at worst, strangled in the undergrowth because of it) and carefully put down his gun. He then put both hands around Tom's neck, picked him up by the ruff, completely off the ground, and shook him, at the same time looking him in the eye and admonishing his disobedience.

This had the desired effect and Tom was once again scrupulous in paying heed to his master. George, meanwhile, picked up his gun, checking the barrels for any obstructions since they had rested on soft earth, and continued walking. He had plenty of shooting, avoiding taking birds going forwards.

All too soon the drive was over and the Guns were driven back to the house on the trailer. Although, technically, this had been the last drive, George and two other Guns stayed behind to flight duck as promised by Charles, once the other Guns had departed.

The Bag

When the trailer arrived at the house, Jem Morgan was just finishing laying out the bag. George asked him for the details and wrote them down for inserting later into his gamebook. He need not have done so because Charles issued cards with the details already inscribed to each Gun. George then quietly asked a Gun, whom he knew shot there regularly, what was considered a proper tip[19].

The final tally was 257 pheasants (171 cocks and 86 hens), 19 brace of grouse, 2½ brace of partridge, 7 woodcock, 14 snipe, 9 mallard, 11 pigeon and 3 rabbits.

As is customary at the end of the day, Jem Morgan went up to each Gun in turn, rather than the other way round, and handed a brace of pheasants to each and woodcock to those who had shot them – George remembered wondering, as a child, why the bag was not divided equally among the Guns since they had shot them after all[20]. The snipe were kept back for Charles. George discreetly shook hands with the keeper, as did the others, palming several notes across into his hand as he did so.

As always at this moment at the end of a shoot, he recalled his father's words: 'When you tip the keeper, don't tip him with anything other than a note; coins are for cabbies. And don't wave the tip around . . . pass it across in the palm of your hand as you shake hands. And if you've had a good day, don't stint yourself . . . show your appreciation with a decent tip. Lord knows, a keeper's wage is a pittance and besides, if you see him right, he'll see you right the next time you're invited to shoot if you're that lucky. In fact, he might even help get you invited again . . . Oh, and by the way, don't be bashful about going to thank the beaters personally. You've no idea how such a simple gesture is appreciated and that one's free to boot!'

Once they had been given their brace each, the Guns thanked Charles and departed, leaving Charles, George, two other Guns and the keeper. The keeper was rehanging the bag on the racks in the back of his Landrover, to take it to his game larder, which was a cool room attached at the back of his cottage. The next day, he would take them to the local game dealer.

Notes: (19) Unless you have been quite specifically told not to by your host or shoot captain, you will be expected to tip the keeper. Beaters will be paid off separately. If you have bought the day through an agent you should ask him what is an appropriate tip, otherwise ask a regular member of the shoot. Only ask your host if none of the other Guns know the answer. As to amount, there is no hard and fast rule.

(20) Once each Gun has been given a brace and other favours fulfilled, the rest of the bag will be sold to a butcher or a game dealer, the income going towards running the shoot.

The Duck Flight

The light was beginning to fade as Charles led the Guns down to the flighting pond which was about 400 yards from the house. Everybody was under strict instructions to keep their dogs on the lead, silence being essential[21].

When they were close enough to the pond – actually it was more of a small lake – to see the lie of the land but not to be seen, Charles quietly and quickly outlined his plan and a few points of safety.

'Don't shoot anything until you're in position and then only if it is coming in. Do be careful not to shoot each other. I know it is obvious, but in the gloom it's natural to shoot much lower than one realises. This could result in another Gun being hit directly by shot or, as often happens I gather, by a ricochet off the water. To be shooting that low really is dangerous anyway. Don't leave your stand until you hear my signal of two whistle blasts, indicating no more shooting, or else you could be shot since you can't be seen in a place where you're not supposed to be.

'I apologize if I'm teaching you to suck eggs but I'm sure you understand my concern. The other thing is, don't shoot at coots or moorhens as they always seem to fly too low anyway. Nuisance as they are, it'll put off any duck if they hear shooting before they're in range. Right, that's all I've got to say . . . any questions? If not, I'll now place each of you in turn.'

Charles took each Gun to his position beside the pond, taking pains to point out where the other Guns would be and the most likely flightpath of the duck.

George settled Tom so that he was not in the way. Had it been wet, he would have taken a small groundsheet so that the dog did not run the risk of rheumatism in later life. He was always diligent in drying off Tom if he ever got wet. Rather than rubbing him with a towel, a process that temporarily removed much of the coat's natural oils, he used an all-enveloping towelling bag.

Having organized his dog, George then oriented himself, checked his arcs of fire, placed two sticks as arc markers and prepared to wait for the duck, wishing he had a shooting stick which would have been perfect for such a situation. Before setting off for the pond, George had put his gun in a sleeve which meant that, if he dropped it, he would not run the risk of fouling the barrels in the dark.

As the light faded, he became restless even though he had only been waiting for half an hour. In the dark there is always a false doubt that perhaps everybody has gone home and left one behind. When should one shoot? Is it best to leave the singleton which often appears first as if reconnoitring for the main flight?[22] All these thoughts and more can play tricks on the mind, leaving the Gun confused and apt to do something careless and rushed when something suddenly appears out of the darkness. This was why George continually maintained a constant 360-degree vigil, which tended to give him a stiff neck but at least kept him alert.

Also, to break the monotony, he occasionally checked his barrels for obstructions. Initially he blew gently down them, but thereafter held them up to the sky where there was just enough ambient light to reflect down the barrels.

His patience was eventually rewarded when he heard the faint but unmistakeable noise of mallards' wings moving through the air, a sort of cross between a hum and a whoosh. He craned to catch a glimpse of them, counting twelve dark shapes circling before straightening up and preparing to land. They were faint, black silhouettes against a slightly less black sky. He fired twice and was rewarded with the noise of two smacks as two birds hit the water to his front.

He had just reloaded when he saw the quicker, silent, dark, small shape of a teal coming in to land. He fired, and killed the teal. By this time the other Guns were all firing. After five minutes there were no more shots but Charles waited another quarter of an hour before blowing his whistle; fifteen minutes that taxed Tom's patience to the absolute limit. Once the whistle had gone, George sent Tom into the water.

By the time they had finished, the bag was nine mallard and

five teal. George adored teal, especially roasted at breakfast after being stuffed the previous night with port-soaked bread.

The Guns met up and made their way back to the house. Before departing, they had a drink with their host who generously gave each a teal and a couple of mallard. George zipped Tom into his towelling bag before lifting him into the car, Tom being somewhat immobile while ensconced in the bag. It was not Tom's favourite item because it was so restrictive; nevertheless this drawback was more than compensated for by its warmth and cosiness[23].

Notes: (21) Duck are arguably the most sensitive of all birds to danger and, consequently even greater care has to be taken when moving into position. If any duck are disturbed on the way in and not shot at, there is a good chance they will return a little later.

(22) One school of thought – the author's mainly – holds that incoming duck send a scout or pair of them, to reconnoitre a pond before coming into feed and settle for the night. If all seems well, or the scouts are shot and not able to return with any news, the rest will come in, seemingly on the basis that no news is good news. If the scouts are shot at but are missed, and return with bad news, the flight will go elsewhere. This credits duck with sophisticated intelligence, which is doubtful. Nevertheless, whether true or not, it is a point to ponder while awaiting an evening flight.

(23) Towelling dog bags are very effective for drying off wet dogs. Many dogs, because of the unnatural restraint on movement, instinctively dislike being put in a bag. Nevertheless, once in, they seem to thoroughly enjoy the experience. The dog is zipped into the bag and his body warmth quickly heats up the air in the bag. Any wetness is convected through the towelling and most dogs should be virtually dry in less than an hour. Any dirt and mud tends to be removed also.

Later

As soon as he arrived home, George checked Tom for thorns, scratches and ailments before feeding him. After hanging his pheasants, he mixed a generous whisky and soda, before setting to cleaning his gun. Once the gun was clean, he cleaned and put away his other equipment before having a good soak in the bath.

When he came down from his bath he wrote up his gamebook and then wrote a thank-you letter to Charles Chute-Strait. In particular, he praised the organization and the variety, and emphasized both his and Tom's appreciation for his host's generosity. He preferred to write immediately because the day was still fresh in his mind and, more importantly, it showed that he appreciated his host's thoughtfulness and consideration; nothing was ruder, to his mind, than the late letter sent many days or even weeks later, which implied a cavalier casualness and lack of real appreciation of a kindness bestowed.

He went to bed feeling very satisfied with a wonderful day. Just as he was about to go to sleep, he realized with pleasure that he had managed to equal the Feudal Park record of the number of game species shot in a day.

2

THE BEGINNER

A Father's Advice

If a sportsman true you'd be,
Listen carefully to me.

Never, never let your gun
Pointed be at anyone;
That it may unloaded be
Matters not the least to me.

When a hedge or fence you cross,
Though of time it cause a loss,
From your gun the cartridge take
For the greater safety's sake.

If 'twixt you and neighbouring gun
Bird may fly or beast may run,
Let this maxim e'er be thine:
'Follow not across the line.'

Stops and beaters, oft unseen,
Lurk behind some leafy screen;
Calm and steady always be;
'Never shoot where you can't see.'

Keep your place and silent be;
Game can hear, and game can see;
Don't be greedy. Better spared
Is a pheasant, than one shared.

You may kill, or you may miss,
But at all times think of this –
'All the pheasants ever bred
Won't repay for one man dead.'

This chapter is not just for the beginner, young and old, but also for the beginner's tutor, for use as a memory jogger. It does not pretend to be completely foolproof but should provide a fairly thorough basis for tuition. A good start for all beginners, and indeed the more experienced, if they do not know it, is to memorize the above poem.

Written in 1909 by Mark Beaufoy MP for his son Henry, on reaching thirteen, it encapsulates all the essential safety points of shooting.

Safety

The chapter on safety in this book says enough, hopefully. Safety, though, is the foundation of all shooting tuition. As Major John Ruffer, author and renowned shooting coach used to maintain, a person can be taught to shoot perfectly in ten shots –it is just that most people fail to do what they have been taught thereafter. Thus, the mechanics of shooting are actually but one small facet of learning to shoot.

The Quarry

Too often people shoot without a thought for their quarry. It is only a fortunate few who can benefit from accompanying a professional keeper throughout the season to learn about game, rearing game, respect for game, and shooting lore in general. Even then, fewer still learn to respect the environment in which the game lives, as is very much the case in Germany, for example.

In Germany, the shooting environment, almost invariably forest, is tended and treated with some reverence – the Forstmeister or head forester of a district is held in similar (or greater) esteem than, say, a General Practitioner in Great Britain. The Germans believe that if one looks after the environment Nature will take its course and game will flourish accordingly and be better for it. There is much merit in this philosophy, relying as it does on wild rather than reared game.

In Great Britain, we have destroyed much 'of our forests and had to plant special coverts just to hold birds. We have not planted the coverts for the improvement of the environment necessarily, but rather in order to be able to provide cover for an artificially reared quarry.

Thus it is essential that the beginner should learn as much about game species, pest species and protected species as possible before shooting any game. At the risk of being repetitive, a German is not allowed to shoot without a permit, which can only be obtained after expensive, long and detailed formal teaching in all aspects of game shooting. While they might not shoot any better (indeed, Germans are more oriented towards ground game than feathered game) at least, theoretically, they know a great deal about their sport. Whether or not we should adopt a similar system is not in the remit of this book. Nevertheless, it will be necessary if newcomers to gameshooting are not properly prepared beforehand, either through their own efforts or someone else's tuition; after all, it is necessary to train in order to obtain a driving licence for driving a motor vehicle which is no more or less dangerous than a shotgun.

The Young Beginner

With luck the young beginner or child will have the benefit of a father or other experienced adult tutor from whom to learn shooting lore. With a child, there is usually so much more time in which to learn – the author began to get his three-year-old son to take him through the steps to be taken on arrival home after a day's shooting. In this way, care of gun and dog, and attention to safety, will hopefully be second nature. Some teaching guidelines follow.

It is natural for sons to want to emulate their fathers but, if a child is patently not interested in guns, do not press the point. Fortunately, children who like playing with guns, once taught, tend also to enjoy demonstrating how to handle them.

Start as young as possible – the author fired an air rifle at the age of seven. Instructing a pupil is also the best way to repolish one's own skills.

When a child is able to manage a whole day in the shooting field, let him accompany you, unarmed, to see what happens, having cleared it with your host first. All the better in some respects, incidentally, if he occasionally sees things that should not happen.

Later on, take the child along as a shadow, carrying an empty gun all day but going through the motions as if the gun was loaded, e.g. taking out the cartridges before crossing an obstacle. The author's grandfather underwent such a grounding for two seasons before being allowed to load his gun. Two seasons may be excessive, but the point is that no person should be allowed into the shooting field with a loaded gun unless he is as safe as can reasonably be expected.

Do not let a child shoot game until he is totally confident with his gun, able to hit clays accurately and consistently, and able to judge consistently and accurately what is a suitable range at which to shoot birds.

Once a child is shooting, do not tolerate any lapses in behaviour, particularly regarding safety. Any lapses in safety must result in going back to carrying an empty gun for a trial period in order to emphasize the value of safety **and** that shooting is a privilege, not a right.

The Adult Beginner

The adult beginner is at a disadvantage since, very often, he does not have the chance to learn shooting lore over a period of years; at worst, he may be trying to learn shooting within a few days or less in order to fulfil an invitation to shoot. He can go to any shooting school and learn how to fire a gun reasonably accurately, but he is unlikely to learn much else except a few essential points of safety. Unfortunately, it will probably not be practical to undergo the sort of training for a child as described above. The following is the best advice, albeit limited, that can be offered.

Under no circumstances, if a complete novice, should you accept an invitation unless you are sure that you can fit in some formal coaching at a shooting school beforehand. If time permits, or if, having taken up gameshooting, you really want to approach the subject properly, you should attend a BASC Proficiency Award Scheme course. These courses are outstandingly good and, while they do not turn out instant experts, they do produce an extremely comprehensive foundation on which to build experience. The syllabus includes: Shooting and Conservation; Shotguns and cartridges; Shotgun safety; The Law; Quarry identification; Behaviour in the field; Game shooting; Rough shooting; The role of gundogs; Gamekeeping; The Sport and the future. The address of BASC is in Appendix Two.

Do not be afraid to seek the advice of others and do not be too proud to heed it. Trust others and do not deviate from their advice until you have gained experience and can therefore judge for yourself – at one extreme their advice should stop you from dressing outrageously but more especially from perpetrating a dangerous act.

Go to a shooting school and practise until you are consistently accurate.

Equip yourself only with essentials, bearing firmly in mind that you may not wish to continue shooting after your initial experience. You may need to borrow a gun, but do not borrow one other than from a knowledgeable source or unless it has been checked and certified as being safe – it may not hurt you but could hurt somebody else. For a small fee, you may be able to persuade a gunsmith to hire you a gun, or to check one borrowed from an inexpert source – remember if you borrow it for more than 72 hours that both the lender and yourself must give the appropriate notices to the chief of police concerned within seven days.

If the opportunity presents itself, accompany a friend as often as possible beforehand to learn what a day's shooting involves. As an old military adage says, 'Time spent in reconnaissance is seldom wasted'.

Do not accept an invitation unless you can fulfil your obligations as a guest, i.e. only accept if you can definitely make the day; also, do not be too proud to admit to being totally inexperienced since, in all probability, it will be apparent the moment you set a foot out of your car on arrival at the shoot. Thereafter, if you have any queries ask your host but, if it is during a drive, seek advice from a neighbour, although not once the birds start to come over.

The Ten Commandments

John Marchington, the well-known author and sportsman, composed the 'commandments' below which could form the foundation of all gameshooters' interest in their sport. Time spent learning these and Mark Beaufoy's poem will not be wasted.

1 Be at all times safe.
2 Always strive to achieve clean kills by avoiding over-long range shooting.
3 Retrieve and despatch wounded game as soon as possible.
4 Place the well-being of your dog before your own.
5 Study to be quiet.
6 Avoid greediness, taking neither unsporting shots nor indulging in excessive killing.
7 Avoid selfishness – let others have the sport which is rightly theirs.
8 Never shoot at quarry you cannot completely see.
9 Respect and conserve the natural scene.
10 Regard shooting as a means to an end, not an end in itself.

Shooting With a Pair Of Guns

If a person, when invited to shoot, is told to bring a pair of guns, it means that he can expect a great deal of fast shooting at a very large number of birds. Such days are rare and the beginner is unlikely to be faced with such an opportunity; this short section is included just in case this happens, though.

It will be necessary to take considerably more ammunition than normal. It is impossible to say how much, but take a couple of 250-cartridge packs. Obviously two guns are needed. Dress needs to be smart and formal, in all likelihood. Normally, loaders will be provided by your host, but do check.

In addition to all the paraphernalia you would normally take, a two-gun day is the one occasion when you do not forget your ear defenders. Even using ear defenders, you are unlikely not to have a headache and a sore shoulder at the end of the day.

Technique

If participating in a two-gun day for the first time, it would be imprudent not to seek the advice of an expert with whom you can also practise changing guns. Any good shooting school should be able to help but, before booking a lesson, establish that the school has the necessary expertise. What follows is for right-handers and, in principle, should be reversed for left-handers.

The loader should stand to your right and slightly behind. He will hold your second, loaded gun in his right hand.

Once you have fired your first gun, you apply the safety-catch – this is most important, especially if only one barrel has been fired – and hand it with your right hand to your loader's left hand.

You take the second gun from your loader's right hand with your left hand.

Do not, either of you, try to cut corners as far as safety is concerned. Thus, make sure your loader knows you will only accept a gun from him with the safety-catch at Safe.

At the end of a drive both of you should unload the gun you are holding, and prove it to each other.

To conclude, it is vital that you establish an immediate rapport with your loader, if he is a stranger to you, and let him know precisely what you expect from him. Practise changing guns and perfect your technique before the first drive.

3
THE HOST

Introduction

The success of a day's shooting depends very much on the skill and good manners of the host; or shoot captain, in the case of a syndicate shooting land it has rented. It is not intended to describe in pedantic detail how a host should behave but, rather, to say what a guest should reasonably expect from his host.

There are hosts and hosts, as the following true story illustrates:

A friend of the author's was once asked to shoot somewhere in Berkshire. The invitation included all the details he needed such as timings, where to meet, what to bring, etc. On arrival, he found several other Guns and a good-sized party of beaters already there. After an excellent initial briefing by their host, everybody went and took their respective places for the first drive. Each stand was beautifully pegged and it was quite obvious that a great deal of preparation had gone into the day.

The morning's shooting was thoroughly enjoyable and everybody was in fine form by lunchtime. It was during lunch that the author's friend turned to his host and remarked casually, 'I didn't know that you owned land in Berkshire. I thought all yours was in Sussex.'

'You're absolutely right. No, I saw this land the other day and thought it promised some good shooting so planned a day's shooting accordingly . . .' entirely without the owner's consent, as it turned out.

What Does A Guest Expect From His Host?

His invitation should include a time and place to meet, with sufficiently detailed directions to get there (send an extract of a map if necessary), whether any meals will or will not be provided, whether or not dogs are welcome, whether to bring more than one gun and, if so, whether to bring a loader and whether or not to bring a friend or companion, although if not mentioned it is pretty safe to assume that the invitation does not extend beyond oneself.

At the meet, the host should introduce any strangers.

The initial brief should be firm, positive, unambiguous, precise and concise, so that each Gun knows exactly what the outline plan for the day is, what to shoot and any particular limitations on conduct through the day, including points of safety and the numbering of Guns at stands.

Throughout the day the host should be unobtrusively running the show, being ready to alter plans if necessary – after due consultation with his keeper, a courtesy sometimes forgotten. If he changes his plan, he must remember to inform all who might possibly be affected by the changes.

The unselfish host will devise a system of numbering so that each Gun has equal opportunities of shooting throughout the day. He will also avoid the temptation to put himself in all the best stands, taking his turn with his guests. He will studiously ensure that all guests get something to shoot at.

The host will ensure birds are presented in such a way that they provide a demanding test of skill which is compatible with the ability of the Guns. He should aim for quality of bag and not quantity. It is not in the remit of this book to lay down what is an excessive bag – a few shoots achieve bags of 1500 pheasants and present the most testing shooting over the heads of the finest shots in the country. Whether or not this is an excessive figure (the author is inclined to think that it is), it is very difficult to reconcile with a growing and active anti-bloodsports lobby, albeit one which is often ill-informed and misguided.

At the end of the day the host will ensure shooting stops at least an hour before sunset to allow pickers-up to complete their task before birds go to roost. He (and his keeper) will also ensure that guests leave with a brace of good birds each. He will thank (and pay) the beaters and have a detailed debrief with his keeper thereafter.

It is essential that the host is firm and confident, so that he inspires confidence in his guests. It is perhaps worth remembering that guests, and indeed all present, want to know what they have to do and that, therefore, they expect to be told what to do. Guests and Guns alike also expect their host to take positive steps to maintain safety should safety ever be jeopardized.

The Code Of Good Shooting Practice

In recent years, there have been increasing instances of serious shooting malpractices with regard to a very few commercial shoots. As with anything in life, if something is ruined – in this case the reputation of the gameshooting fraternity – it is almost invariably because of gross misbehaviour by a tiny minority. By this is meant that there are establishments purporting to be shoots when all they are are shooting factories; they survive only because their clients are willing to pay for the entertainment they offer.

The author heard of one agent who had a prospective client who wanted to break the record for the number of partridge falling to one gun in a day. Fortunately, the agent declined to arrange the proposed massacre and the client's ardour cooled anyway on being told of the cost – £52,000 at 1989 prices.

Hence there are too many stories of several-thousand-bird-a-day shoots and partridge days where, for example, the birds are released from boxes into totally unfamiliar territory and channelled, utterly disoriented, down a valley across which are placed the Guns. At the end of each drive, the Guns about-face and shoot at the surviving birds, which are forced back whence they came. As the stock becomes depleted it is recharged by releasing more birds from boxes.

A Code of Good Shooting Practice has been drawn up jointly by the BASC, BFSS and Game Conservancy. This code will only be effective if shoot owners and captains, and gameshooters, abide by it and take positive action to help eliminate any malpractices. Guns must not accept bad behaviour and must, if aware of malpractice, report it to any one of the agencies which drew up the code.

Golden Rules
The Code of Good Shooting Practice is a mixture of objective and subjective judgements and standards.

The objective standards are enshrined in the following principle:

'Rearing and releasing of game for shooting should only be done in order to provide a sufficient stock of game, fully adapted to the wild, which can be sustained without damage to the environment or to the wild stock.'

Three golden rules evolve from this principle:

1 No birds shall be released after the start of annual shooting in the area concerned and they shall not be shot until they are fully adult and well adapted to the wild. Pheasant should be released at least one month before the commencement of shooting, partridge and duck at least fourteen days.

2 No bird previously released shall subsequently be caught up during its shooting season for re-release during that season.

3 No more birds shall be released in an area of woodland, game cover, or pond than the area can hold without detriment to the health of the birds or to the environment.

4
SAFETY

As stated in the Introduction, this book's main aim is to preach safety. While it would be rash to deny the influence of fate, fate usually intervenes only after some form of carelessness. Genuine accidents do happen but, nine times out of ten, they occur due to negligence by someone and, frequently, not on the part of the victim.

There are four areas of safety; the points under each heading are not necessarily in a set order of priority. In order to press the point, this chapter is necessarily clipped and curt, hence the simplest classification of Do's and Don'ts.

Guns and Ammunition

Do maintain and service your gun carefully.

Don't use a gun you know to be unsafe.

Don't buy a gun unless you have a reputable gunsmith's certificate to say that it is in proof and safe.

Don't open a gun after a misfire unless it is pointed well away from people and dogs.

Don't mix different calibres of ammunition in pockets or any other container or dangerous bursts can be caused.

Don't allow ammunition to get too close to dampness or excessive heat.

Do use the correct shot size shot for your intended quarry.

Don't use damaged amunition – remember that a life is worth more than the few pence of a cartridge.

Don't use ammunition which the gun has not been proved for, e.g. Magnum cartridges in standard chambers.

Don't ever be complacent.

On The Road

Do keep guns, and ancillary equipment which might advertise the presence of guns, hidden and protected, especially when the vehicle is unattended. A surprising number of spare guns, left unattended in vehicles during shoots, are stolen each year. You can now be prosecuted for failing to keep your gun secure.

Don't travel with a loaded weapon.

Do lock your vehicle whenever it is unattended.

Don't be complacent.

At Home

Do keep photographs of your gun(s) and records of their serial numbers.

Don't store guns and ammunition together, if possible – this prevents an intruder using your gun on you, or saves a curious child from potential disaster if he or she gets hold of the gun.

Don't leave an assembled gun where children can reach it.

Don't load a gun indoors.

Do lock guns out of sight; ideally in a proper gun cabinet.

Do always check a gun is unloaded before handling it.

Do not be complacent.

In The Field

Don't ever allow a gun to be pointed at anyone whether it is unloaded or not.

Don't carry a gun at the trail – the barrel may be jabbed into the ground or a trigger could be snagged on an obstruction, with fatal consequences.

Don't carry a gun so that it is pointing at anyone.

Don't carry a loaded gun over your shoulder. Avoid doing this with an unloaded gun too (it should be broken or in a sleeve), since it is easy to swing your gun unwittingly into anybody close behind.

Don't shoot ground game to the front on a driven shoot.

Don't ever shoot low birds or those that are too close.

Don't swing down or through the line.

Don't be greedy; rather, choose targets discriminately.

Don't change position once placed. Stand still and remain silent. In the rare event that you are told to move, ensure Guns either side know your new position.

Don't pick up birds half-way through a drive.

Don't ever tie a dog to you.

Don't drink too much – most accidents happen after lunch . . .

Don't fiddle with the safety catch and triggers.

Don't hand a gun to someone without first showing them it is unloaded.

Don't shoot unless the whole target is visible.

Don't shoot into cover.

Don't shoot once the end of a drive has been indicated.

Don't lean a gun against anything (cars, trees, etc.) or leave on top of a car.

Don't knock your barrels or anybody else's, since they dent very easily and can be expensive to rectify.

Don't shoot if unbalanced in any way.

Don't rest the tips of barrels on your feet.

Don't ever load a gun unless you intend to use it, i.e. only load once the drive has started.

Do unload immediately a drive ends.

Do carry your gun over your forearm, open and pointing at the ground. Unless in a sleeve, this is accepted as the best way to carry a gun. Carry it empty, unless you are actually walking up game.

Do frequently check the safety catch is on.

Do check the barrels are clear before loading at the start of each drive.

Do look through the barrels if there is the slightest chance that they are blocked by mud, snow or anything else.

Do close the stock to the barrels and not barrels to stock. This way the barrels are always pointing at the ground, and the cartridges cannot fall out.

Do check the gun is unloaded at the end of a drive and again before putting in a sleeve, case or car.

Do keep a gun broken and empty when in company between drives.

Do remove cartridges before crossing any obstacle such as a stream or fence – merely opening a loaded gun is not sufficient.

Do check a gun is unloaded on receiving it, unless the person handing it over has made this clear already by showing you.

Do point barrels in the air when beaters come into sight towards the end of a drive. This indicates you have seen them and prevents swinging the gun up through them.

Do watch others lest they are dangerous. You may not be able to say much but at least you will be alert to possible dangers.

Do be insured. Membership of BASC automatically gives cover of £2,000,000.

Do listen carefully to your host's or shoot captain's briefings.

Do avoid being complacent; the second you think you're foolproof safe is the moment when you will do something you could regret for evermore.

Every single point mentioned here has been the cause of an accident at some time, some more than others. **Do not** add to the list; it is far too long as it is.

5
CARE OF THE GUN

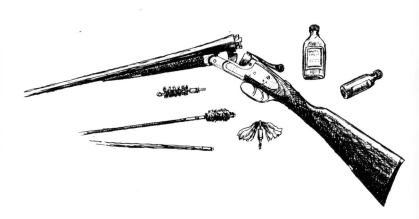

Care of one's gun comes second only to care of one's dog. Gun cleaning should be a rigid discipline that happens as soon as one arrives home after a day's shooting – nothing rusts faster than a gun brought inside damp. A few minutes simple effort may save much unnecessary expense and even life.

Failure to clean a gun will result, almost immediately, in the deposits from fired cartridges in the barrels etching into the steel and causing pitting which weakens the barrels. Water causes instant rust on all bare metal parts but is most dangerous in those crevices under the extractors, in and around the action and either side of the rib. Blood and salt water should be removed the instant they are discovered in the shooting field, since they are about the most corrosive agents likely to be encountered.

What may seem like a tedious and elaborate ritual, on first acquaintance, surprisingly enough soon becomes a quick, simple, satisfying and almost automatic habit. If you care for your gun properly, it should serve you for your and probably your children's lifetimes; if you do not, somebody could be maimed or even killed.

Cleaning Equipment

It is easy to buy a comprehensive cleaning kit very cheaply, which will cover all everyday cleaning needs. Do ensure, though, that you buy the correct sized cleaning kit for the bore of your gun. The following is a comprehensive list of cleaning equipment:

Cleaning rods*
Cleaning rod attachments: Wool mop, Phosphor bronze, Pull-through loop*
Cloth patches*
Oil: thick and thin varieties*
Cotton cleaning rag
Beeswax wood polish

Polishing duster
Paradox gun cleaner
Small, stiff, bristle (not plastic) brush, e.g. a trimmed ½"
paintbrush
Set of turnscrews
Tissues or soft lavatory paper
A clean, dry, safe place for keeping the gun after cleaning

* These items comprise the average cleaning kit set.

Routine/End of Day Cleaning

When cleaning any gun, follow these principles:

1 Prove the gun is unloaded before doing anything else.
2 Strip the weapon to a logical sequence. Since most guns consist of three main parts only, this applies to more than routine stripping and cleaning and, unless the weapon has detachable sidelocks, further stripping will be limited to the extractors. Leave anything else to a gunsmith.
3 Use the correct tools and cleaning equipment correctly.
4 Place weapon components in a clean, dry, safe place.
5 Do not use undue force in dismantling or assembly. Again, this would normally only apply if the weapon is being stripped beyond its main components. If you cannot unscrew a pin (the technical term for a gunscrew) leave it to a gunsmith.

The sequence of cleaning will be:

The Stock

Wipe away any moisture and dirt from the action and wood with a clean cloth. On no account ever rub the woodwork with an oily cloth. Oil rots the woodwork and therefore must be used sparingly on the action so that it does not seep into the woodwork.

If the woodwork is of the oil-finished (linseed type) variety, rubbing a hand over the surface will usually return its appearance to normal again, otherwise apply a little linseed oil.

If the woodwork is french polished, then treat it with best quality furniture polish.

Clean the chequering (intended to aid grip) with a soft bristle brush (the ½″ paint brush).

Wipe exposed parts of the action with a very thin coat of oil, once you have removed any dirt and the deposits which tend to gather on the face of the breech. Even if the gun has got soaked, on no account should you try to inject oil into the action via the firing pin slots. It will not counter the action of any moisture but merely find its way into the woodwork like water into a sponge. If the gun has been properly serviced and stored correctly the internal mechanism will be protected from moisture by a film of grease and moisture will evaporate harmlessly.

The Fore-end

Wipe the woodwork and metal parts with a clean cloth. Use the bristle brush on the chequering if necessary. Wipe the metal parts with a very fine film of oil from an oily but not oil-saturated rag.

The Barrels

Wipe the outside clean and dry, paying particular attention to the rib, since this is a bad water trap – once rust gains a hold, it will eventually cause the rib to separate from the barrels, rendering the gun unsafe.

Remove any dirt from behind the ejectors with a small piece of rag. It is usually sufficient to remove the ejectors (by removing the screw (pin) on the underside of the barrels) once in the middle of, then at the end of the season, and if the gun has been soaked. Using a cotton wool bud or pipecleaner, remove any dirt and moisture from the extractor bed. Oil the parts lightly before replacing them.

Unless you have a Paradox cleaner, an effective method for cleaning the inside of the barrels is as follows. Get three pieces of soft lavatory paper or other tissue and roll into a wad which fits fairly tightly into the chamber. Push the wad through the barrels with your cleaning rods. This will remove all but the most stubborn deposits. Then, using the wool mop or pull-through attachment, lightly oil the barrels. Ensure the tissue wad is a good fit but not too tight, or else you could damage the barrels if you have to use excessive force to push the wad through.

For stubborn deposits, use the phosphor bronze brush, ideally with a cleaning patch wrapped round it. Try to use the phosphor bronze brush sparingly because excessive use could damage the barrels.

Incidentally, always check the fittings on cleaning rods for any proud or burred edges. On no account use damaged rods since they will irreversibly score the barrels.

Wipe the outside of the barrels with a thin film of oil, reassemble and put away the gun.

End-of-Season Cleaning and Preservation

Always clean the gun extra carefully at the end of the season; it is not so much the cleaning as the preservation that is important. Strip and clean the gun normally but ensure the metal is well oiled and wood well polished. Store in a secure, cool, dry, airy place (beware of cellars, though) in its case (ensure it is dry) or, ideally, in a gun cabinet. Avoid storing close to warm radiators, and other sources of heat.

If intending to store a gun assembled, in a gun cabinet, it is logical to place it in the cabinet barrels uppermost. Beware, though: excessive oil, over time, runs downwards and eventually through the firing pin holes into the wood of the stock, where it will cause rot. To obviate this, only oil the barrels lightly and check them from time to time.

Servicing

It is wise to have a gun serviced every two years, unless you have shot very regularly or the gun has got wet, in which cases it should be done every year. Do not economize on this aspect since a gunsmith's inspection may nip a potential (and dangerous) disaster in the bud, which might otherwise only manifest itself at the worst possible moment. An example might be finding rust along the rib, or detecting the effects of rust and wear on firing pins, both things unlikely to be spotted by the owner.

Out-of-Season Cleaning

Check your gun every two months or so and re-oil as necessary. Oil moves, and metalwork could then be exposed to humidity and rust.

6
DRESS AND EQUIPMENT

Your intentions, when dressing and equipping yourself, should be to be comfortable, to blend in comfortably with your natural surroundings and to conform with your companions. Rather in the way that a person joins a club on its terms, so the guest has a certain obligation to conform to his host's desires within the bounds of common sense and propriety.

While this chapter will help the beginner to avoid that minefield which is littered with opportunities for self-embarrassment, it is not a failsafe for those with an unerring eye for the unconventional. It should be pointed out at this stage that while it is not smart to look deliberately scruffy, dressing in completely new kit from top to toe also causes a person to be conspicuous.

The British tend to draw some comfort from things that are old and well-established, be it their stately homes, their family heirlooms, best English guns or whatever. Such things have an intrinsic value in that they are tried, tested and have proved their reliability and trustworthiness. Anything new is unproven and therefore, until it has proved itself, it will often be treated with varying degrees of suspicion and diffidence. The beginner, therefore, can help himself (and his confidence) by not looking too fresh from the factory.

Dress

Headwear

A hat serves several purposes. It can prevent the loss of 40% of the wearer's body heat; it will camouflage the balding or snowy tonsure and, finally, it will offer protection from the wind, rain and sun. The standard flat cap is *de rigeur* – simple and without embellishment and definitely not the launch-pad variety favoured by pre-war golfers. Avoid also porkpies, deerstalkers and sou'westers which are not really suitable. If your jacket comes with a hood, make sure it can be detached and do so. Hoods narrow your vision, impede your hearing and are therefore potentially dangerous.

Ears

It is strongly recommended that some form of ear defender is worn while shooting. Ear defenders vary from the headphone type to simple foam ear-plugs. The headphone type is perfectly acceptable and efficient but can be cumbersome; buy green or brown, or else birds may avoid you! Almost as good these days are the foam plugs which are twisted to a point between finger and thumb and inserted into the ear where they expand to form a perfect fit; also, they are very cheap. Remember that ear defenders' purpose is to eliminate the damaging decibel frequencies only, thereby allowing the wearer to hear other sounds, especially voices. It is unwise to spend too much since even the most expensive plugs will eventually harden up due to the effects of wax and be rendered useless.

While careful consideration should be given to wearing anything that interferes with the senses of sight, hearing and smell, it is a well-proven fact that shooting causes deafness if ears are unprotected. Hearing in the left ear will be affected first in the person who shoots off his right shoulder and vice versa, since this will be the ear most exposed to muzzle blast.

Face

By all means wear a silk or woollen scarf in extremes of weather. Balaclavas and variants are out, not least because, like hoods, they inhibit the senses. It is possible too to try too hard to blend in. Hence military face-veils (which also double as scarves) should be avoided; apart from other considerations, they scratch and snag easily when walking through thick undergrowth. Nevertheless, they are very useful for wildfowling and pigeon flighting and are recommended for these activities.

Neck

Much depends on the weather and the occasion as to what is appropriate to wear around the neck. Except in a heatwave or when rough shooting, it is sensible to wear a collar and tie.

Although it might seem rather formal, such a combination is extraordinarily effective at keeping the wearer warm in a breeze and reasonably dry in the rain. A Viyella shirt with a conservative tie is ideal. It is not unknown for a tie to come in useful to secure a splint for a broken limb, but it human or canine.

An item worth carrying in a spare pocket is a towelling cravat. While it could be worn anyway on an informal day, it really comes into its own in wet weather, when it soaks up the rain and yet is still warm and comfortable.

Coat/Jacket

This is the one item not to stint on. On all but the most formal days (and then depending on the weather) the choice is enormous. The very formal day still requires a traditional tweed suit consisting of jacket, waistcoat, breeches, shooting stockings and stout leather shoes or brogues. While there are new materials appearing all the time which claim a host of magical qualities, there is still nothing quite as versatile as waxed, thornproof cotton. Such garments have their faults and are not necessarily perfect for every weather condition but there is nothing that is remotely as good all round.

Again, it is possible to spend a fortune; all that should be said is that false economy is foolish and it is wise to buy the very best that you can afford. There are several brands of waxed jacket available of which Barbour is the best known and, arguably, the best – it may be the most expensive available but not by much and it really lives up to its makers' claims, whereas few others even come close. Debatably, the Rolls-Royce of jackets is the quilted tweed shooting jacket made by Husky, well-known for their quilted jackets, which they will make up in the tweed of your choice. Basically, this jacket is tweed, lined with man-made thermal quilting and a water-resistant inner layer.

Avoid expensive Loden cloth garments which, while out-standingly warm and long-lasting, are heavy, bulky and not suitable for the speed of reaction required to shoot feathered game. They are perfect for boar shoots in the raw winter weather found in Central Europe, but too restrictive for most other forms of shooting.

Essentially a shooting jacket should: be designed for game-shooting (as opposed to clay-pigeon or skeet shooting); be warm; be rainproof but not totally waterproof, since such a garment would induce perspiration, although Gore-tex comes remarkably close to providing the perfect solution; be comfortable and, therefore, large enough to allow free movement when wielding a gun; be sober in colour (green or brown) and free of badges. Finally, it should have plenty of pockets, the main ones strong enough to carry loose cartridges repeatedly without wearing through.

Incidentally, most waxed cotton jackets are supplied with a belt. Here again snobbery creeps in, but this can be substituted by sound logic. Belts are not customarily worn outside jackets (this includes cartridge belts) since they snag easily and they prevent the wearer from getting to the inside pockets quickly without half undressing and putting down his gun, which should be avoided when possible. At the same time, a belt also reduces the gap between the inside of the jacket and the next garment and therefore restricts the circulation of warm air generated by the body. In wet weather, the belt also acts as a tiresome rain trap.

Underneath

The layer principle should apply, when dressing for shooting, on the basis that several thin layers are better than a few thick ones. The aim must be to be comfortable but able to move freely. Encumbrances must be minimized to allow quick and free movement with a gun in the shoulder.

In cold weather, a quilted waistcoat is useful as a thermal lining. Under this, particularly if there is much walking to be done, there should rarely be very much need for more than a lambswool pullover, a shirt and maybe a vest; the quilted waistcoat can often be dispensed with.

In very cold conditions or for those with thin blood or bad hangovers, thermal underwear can be beneficial. Thermals, as they are known, should be made from a wool and cotton and/or silk mix, with a small percentage of man-made fibre for strength – they should be thin, light and cellular in construction. It does not necessarily follow that you need to wear both a thermal vest and leggings. A thermal vest should only be necessary if you are likely to be standing for long periods in the sort of conditions that keep polar bears indoors.

Hands

It is extremely dangerous to shoot with hands so cold that they fumble. Gloves, like towelling cravats, should be kept permanently in a recess of one's shooting coat so that they are never left behind. Whether leather or woollen, the trigger finger should be cut away to leave the top two joints free to operate the triggers; most shooting gloves are designed thus these days.

Leather gloves can be a misery in wet weather unless they are lined in some way, ideally with a separate silk liner. This is where the woollen glove excels. It is just as warm as leather but, when wet, still keeps the hands warm due to the natural insulating properties of wool. Some woollen gloves have leather sewn into the palms, which aids grip and is recommended.

Breeches

Ordinary trousers tucked into wellingtons are fine for dry conditions but act like a drainpipe in the rain by channelling water into the feet of wellingtons. Breeches are more practical in all conditions – cooler on a hot day and infinitely better in the wet.

Breeches or breeks traditionally used to be styled as plus-fours. These days, plus-fours have largely given way to plus-twos, the number referring to the extra inches required to produce an overhang of material. The overhang is a catchment for any water absorbed by the material and ensures that it drips outside one's boots or not down one's socks if wearing shoes.

As with the rest of the shooting wardrobe, breeches should be loose fitting to allow for easy movement, greater warmth and general comfort, but not excessively so. A good, strong, conservative tweed is recommended since it offers warmth, longevity, smartness and resistance to snagging and precipitation but, once soaked, can be most uncomfortable. Equally practical for informal days are breeches made from moleskin or corduroy, moleskin being far the better of the two.

Lederhosen, as favoured on the Continent, especially in Germany, are wonderful and virtually indestructible – so much so that they are often passed from generation to generation. Their major failing, though, is that when soaked they render walking as easy as walking knee-deep through wet cement; for this reason in particular, they are not recommended for wearing in the British climate.

Socks/Stockings

Shooting socks or stockings should be long enough to provide a generous overlap between their tops and the hems of the breeches. When worn with shoes and therefore exposed to view, they should be restrained in hue and pattern. If hidden inside wellingtons, the colour matters little, within reason, and the extrovert can express himself more or less as he pleases. The best socks are predominantly woollen with a small percentage of man-made fibre to prolong wear.

Leggings/Waterproof Trousers

Leggings are literally that, consisting of a tube for each leg linked by ties. Trousers are more convenient and offer better protection. Again, waxed thornproof is ideal. An alternative might be trousers of rubberised nylon, Gore-tex or similar man-made fibre. Man-made fibre, though, is noisier than natural fibres, rustling with each step. This can be most irritating when silence is called for, especially when moving into position to flight duck.

Footwear

In warm, dry conditions, a stout walking shoe is recommended since wellingtons make feet sweat. For walking across rugged terrain, it is better to wear walking boots rather than shoes since they afford better ankle support. Puttees with shoes are an alternative of course.

Otherwise, wellingtons are now the most popular footwear. There is no doubt that the most versatile wellington is the green 'Hunter' by virtue of its flexibility and lightness. The main disadvantage of wellingtons, as mentioned, is that they cause sweaty feet. This can be overcome to a large extent by buying oversize boots to allow the comfortable wearing of two or even three pairs of socks. Such a combination absorbs moisture, keeps the feet dry and provides good insulation in cold conditions.

Beware, though, of too thick socks. Ideally a thin inner pair should accompany a thickish pair. If your feet feel too tight in your boots, they will be highly prone to cold because blood flow will be restricted and there will be no air pocket to be warmed by the feet.

As with everything else, it is possible to be extravagant and go for a leather-lined 'super welly' which can even, in extremis, be tailored to fit the leg. They are outstandingly comfortable but cost five or six times more than the 'Hunter'. By virtue of their leather lining, sweaty feet are almost eliminated.

Equipment

Theoretically, once equipped, the game shot should be set up for life. There should be no need to replace the essentials or hardwear items of his inventory, such as guns and cartridge bags, unless he succumbs to self-indulgence or used a false economy in the first place. Like any interest though, there is never a dearth of new gadgets which, once bought, become instantly indispensable. Self-restraint should be the novice's maxim: it is idiotic to spend a small fortune only to decide that you dislike shooting after one day's shooting.

The list of equipment that follows is arranged in alphabetical order and each item is annotated either E for Essential, D for Desirable/Useful, or L for Luxury.

Cartridges (E)

Buy the best you can afford. The cheapest cartridges can represent a false economy and are more likely to perform badly and cause pitting inside barrels. Certainly, cartridges of British origin are pretty satisfactory.

Cartridge Bag (E)

A cartridge bag full of cartridges will be adequate for most days and is a convenient way of carrying up to a hundred cartridges, bearing in mind that fifty may be comfortable to carry but a hundred is another matter altogether. Many Guns put enough cartridges in a pocket until they are likely to meet up with their cartridge bag again, rather than lugging the whole lot from drive to drive; not easy if towing a dog, carrying a gun and sundry other impedimenta. Only buy leather or canvas bags since plastic ones do not 'breathe' and retain moisture, which is anathema to cartridges.

It is sensible to buy a bag with a canvas shoulder strap rather than a leather strap which adds to the weight, particularly if wet, and is less comfortable than canvas. It is wise, too, to have your initials embossed on the oval part of the securing strap on the flap of the bag, for easy recognition among several other bags in the back of a trailer, Landrover or whatever other shoot transport is provided. Another means of identification is to have a saddler replace the canvas strap with a distinctive one of your own; regimental stable belts are a perfect substitute, for example.

Cartridge Belt (D)

If worn, a cartridge belt is always worn under a jacket unless rough shooting – apart from anything else, this protects the cartridges from the elements and eliminates the tell-tale reflection from their bases. A cartridge belt provides a handy reserve – it is impossible to predict cartridge expenditure and twenty-five cartridges (the average contents of a box and capacity of the average belt) is a very useful reserve for unexpected quantities of birds.

A belt should be leather with a generous strap to allow for extra layers of clothing or seasonal over-indulgence. Closed loops are preferable to open loops since cartridges cannot slip through accidentally.

Cartridge Magazine (L)
A cartridge magazine looks like a small suitcase or attaché case with compartments. Although heavy, they enable one to keep cartridges with different loads or shot size separately, i.e. heavier loads for duck flighting with No. 4 or 5 and No. 6, No. 7, etc. for game shooting. Different calibre cartridges, e.g. 12 and 20 bore, should not be carried in the same magazine. They are only really useful for a two-gun day with loaders, since they allow quicker access to cartridges when reloading, and are the most effective way to carry large numbers of cartridges. The average magazine holds 250.

Cleaning Kit (E)
Do not stint on your cleaning kit – cheap cleaning rods could result in barrels irreparably scored by badly-finished fittings. Cleaning kits containing rods, phosphor bronze brush, sheepskin brush or wool mop, pull-through, patches and oil cost a few pounds only; obviously each item is available individually.

A very effective and most highly recommended additional item is a Paradox cleaning rod. This is a rod enveloped in washable nylon fur which is quite remarkable in the way that it removes the heaviest deposits; it also has the advantage that it is virtually impossible to scratch the barrels in any way with it.

First Aid Kit (E)
An item carried by relatively few people, it is not so much for

humans as for dogs which injure themselves on wire or other sharp objects. A screw-top cigar tube is an ideal container for: needle, thread, antiseptic (such as Gentian Violet or liquid Savlon) and cotton wool.

Game Bag (D)

An essential item for the rough shooter likely to kill a lot of game, or for walking Guns unaccompanied by armies of beaters. Traditional game bags are canvas with a net pouch on the outside and a strong, wide canvas shoulder strap.

Game Book (D)

A game book is a historical record of a sportsman's shooting career, showing where and when he shot what with whom, plus a brief description of each day. It should not be treated as merely a tally to be added to at every opportunity.

Game Carriers (D)

Rather more common on the Continent, they are a less convenient alternative, or addition even, to the Game Bag. Carriers are leather thongs which hang from the belt and to which game is attached by the neck. Those who lack height tend to find game carried thus drags along the ground! After a while, walking becomes awkward for even the tallest, particularly if more game is added.

Guns (E)

Countless volumes are available already on the subject of guns. Nevertheless, it is so important that it is necessary to devote more than just passing comment to the matter.

Type It is essential to buy the right gun for the right occasion. In the same way that a table tennis bat is unsuitable for tennis, so a pump-gun is inappropriate for a formal, driven pheasant shoot. As explained in the Glossary, play safe and buy a side-by-side shotgun which will not be out of place on any occasion whether it be a game or clay pigeon shoot.

(At this juncture it is worth pointing out that, while they are perfectly acceptable and have a strong following, over-and-unders and other non-side-by-side guns are frowned upon in certain game shooting circles; even though most people who frown on them have no idea why they do except that it seems to be the thing to do. Over-and-unders can be heavier to carry and more awkward to hold than conventional side-by-side guns while waiting at a stand for game to appear. Unlike a side-by-side, an over-and-under may be difficult to hold in the crook of the arm facing downwards unless it is broken, which can result in longer reloading times compared to a side-by-side. Thus the owner might have to hold his weapon with both hands, which becomes uncomfortable after a while and can lead to holding it in a position that is potentially dangerous to neighbouring Guns.)

If buying second-hand, avoid hammer guns which demand even higher standards of care and alertness from the user. Hammer guns started to go out of fashion at the beginning of the twentieth century but are still available.

Bore Size The majority of gameshots use 12 bores, although 16 bores are usually lighter and nearly as effective, while 20 bores are lighter still.

Weight takes on greater significance with advancing years. The key advantage of a 12 bore is that it can fire a heavier charge of shot, something which is important if wildfowling, for example. Also, in an emergency, you are likely to be able to buy or borrow 12 bore cartridges more readily than any other size.

Make Some of the best shotguns are made in Great Britain as, indeed, are some of the most expensive. Other countries, particularly, Spain and Italy make extremely good guns which, while much cheaper and not sharing the same cachet as English guns, could last an owner's and his children's lifetimes, with care. If you can possibly afford it, buy a gun with ejectors; a gun without them is a real hindrance on a busy drive.

Cost 'You gets what you pay for' holds very true when buying a gun. In 1990, it is possible to pay £30,000 for a new Purdey (many people buy them in pairs). A made-to-measure W. & C. Scott boxlock costs about £6,000. An AYA sidelock costs about £1,200 and an AYA boxlock, depending on embellishment, between £400 and £900. It is possible to pay as little as £200 for a side-by-side but 'you gets what you pays for . . .' Buy the best you can afford.

Safety It is an offence to use, sell or offer for sale a gun that is out of proof or unsafe in any way. Unless buying from a reputable dealer or maker, it is essential to seek the advice of a professional gunsmith before paying for a gun.

Fitment If a gun does not fit, it could result in consistently poor shooting. Even an eighth of an inch too much or too little in the stock can make all the difference. Most gunsmiths can alter stocks easily. Incidentally, when being measured, wear your normal shooting attire, i.e. waxed cotton or other jacket.

Gun Cabinet (E/D)

Gun cabinets may become a legal requirement as part of owning a gun; currently they are not under the Firearms (Amendment) Act 1988, even though some police forces are insisting that private firearms must now be kept in them. If that is not the case, the Police will still be more inclined to issue a shotgun certificate if they know a gun will be secured in a cabinet. Cabinets can also be wired into burglar alarm systems. There is no particular brand which stands out; buy the strongest you can afford. While not always feasible – and some cabinet manufacturers make a point of including ammunition storage space – try to avoid storing ammunition in the same place as guns.

Gun Case (E)

It is ludicrous to spend a fortune on a gun and then not keep it carefully. Gun cases range from the moulded plastic variety to hand-made leather and oak. Plastic cases are more easily damaged, whereas leather-covered wooden cases tend to be

71

able to take remarkable battering but are very heavy. Virtually all gun cases have compartments for cleaning equipment.

Gun Sleeve (D)
If a shoot involves much getting into and out of vehicles, a sleeve (sometimes called a slip or cover) is recommended to reduce the chances of damage to the gun; it also saves walking about with an open gun and virtually eliminates the chance of an accidental discharge. Try to avoid plastic sleeves since they prevent air circulating, thereby encouraging rust and rot in damp conditions. Fleece-lined leather covers are nice but expensive. A lined, heavy-duty canvas or waxed cotton sleeve is very adequate. Whether you buy a sleeve with a full length zip or a flap at the stock end is a matter of preference. Zips can be awkward if wet, rusty or damaged and render the sleeve utterly useless if so, whereas the flap type can be more easily mended *in situ.*

Never store a gun in its sleeve since the risk of damage from moisture is very serious, whatever material the sleeve is made from. Always dry a sleeve after use, especially if there has been moisture about.

Hip-flask (L)
As mentioned already, a hip-flask is a good social ice-breaker but bear in mind that the contents are apt to dull the senses.

Heat/Hand Guards (L)
These slide over the barrels to protect the leading hand from blistering on hot barrels. They are necessary mainly when firing a lot of cartridges in rapid succession, such as during a shooting lesson or for large-bag days which do not warrant two guns per person.

Knife (E)
You might never need it but you will be enormously grateful you carried one should you have cause to use it. A small, sharp,

wooden-handled, French Opinel pocket-knife is ideal. These knives are versatile enough to gralloch a deer in emergency – the author once had to do this when he came across a severely injured deer on a pheasant shoot and was most grateful for his knife – or to administer the picnic.

Shooting Stick (D)
Not really necessary unless you are slightly infirm or injured, and expecting to be a long time waiting at stands. Something of a nuisance to carry if already encumbered by gun, game and dog.

Torch (E)
Essential only really if wildfowling. These days there are several small but impressively efficient torches about, the metal bodied ones being able to double as a Priest. Whatever you buy, ensure it is waterproof.

Whistle (E)
Only essential for dog owners and wildfowlers. A whistle (unless it is of dubiously useful 'Silent' type) is more likely to carry further than the voice, which could make all the difference to a wildfowler trapped in mud. 'ACME Thunderers', police whistles and other mass-produced whistles with identical tones should be avoided, since they are too intrusive or likely to be used by keepers and shoot captains on occasion, to indicate the start and finish of drives. Hand-made bone whistles, for example, are ideal, each having its own unique tone which will not result in a plethora of confused dogs when blown.

Wristwatch (E)
This is mentioned in the very unlikely event that somebody might not carry one. Apart from anything else, a watch is essential as an aid to arriving at a shoot on time; it is unforgivable to arrive late at a shoot. Unlike most other social events, it is

essential to turn up early to a shoot so as not to ruin the host's carefully laid plans. A watch is equally essential for the wildfowler to keep abreast of the tidal situation, since in the dark it is very difficult to know what the state of the tide is.

This chapter has attempted to give a balanced ideal of what is safe to wear in the shooting field. False economy could cost life. In the case of clothing, the loss of life would probably be confined to the wearer. This may sound alarmist but it is true, especially for the wildfowler.

The effects of errors in one's choice of attire may only manifest themselves years later through rheumatism and arthritis. It is sensible therefore to look after oneself and never take the weather for granted. Whatever the case, if you look after yourself it will go some way to making you a safer shot.

7
DOGS

This chapter offers broad advice only. Each heading warrants a separate book and almost certainly will have a book on it already. The chapter deals with gun dogs only.

When one considers how little a dog costs and how much it does for its owner, it offers the best value for money imaginable; that is, as long as its master shows and tells it exactly what is required of it. So often, dogs are expected to be clairvoyant as to their masters' demands and are belaboured for inevitably failing. Ultimately, a dog can only be as good as its handler/master.

Which Breed?

Unless an expert in a particular breed, it may be wise to avoid rarer, more exotic breeds of gun dog. Rare breeds are more likely to be inbred, highly-strung, difficult to handle and unpredictable towards other people. The breeds mentioned here will be confined to Labradors, Retrievers, Spaniels, Pointers and Setters, although the last two are really for the expert or specialist.

Points to Look For

When choosing any dog, look for a combination of the following: fearlessness; its reaction to sudden noise – is it likely to be gun-shy?; good coat; straight legs; broad head; good wagging tail; bright eyes and friendly disposition. Avoid: over-excited dogs; timidity; dogs with very pale eyes (this is the author's prejudice since it often seems to indicate a shifty, untrustworthy animal, but is not a hard and fast rule); inbreeding (look at the pedigree).

Follow your instincts, since you will almost immediately sense whether an animal may be right or wrong. Before completing a deal, insist on a vet's examination. A vet will be able to pick up such hereditary defects as Retinitis and Hip Dysplasia (which is common in inbred Labradors). One owner of the author's acquaintance managed to get a refund when his ten-year-old Labrador developed Hip Dysplasia. This was an exceptional case and the breeder must have been very big-hearted (or terrified) to accept responsibility at this stage of the dog's life.

Working Strain

If going for a pedigree dog, make sure it is bred from working stock and not show stock. A Crufts Champion is bred for showing and may well cringe at the mere mention of shooting. A study of a dog's pedigree will reveal the right signs by the prefixes FTCh (Field Trial Champion) and FTW (Field Trial Winner) in front of the Kennel Name, e.g. FTCh Victrix of Shermill. There is little doubt that dogs inherit skills or aptitudes. Thus a long line of FTChs is a good indicator of inherent ability; it is far from a guarantee though.

Do you really need a pedigree dog? Are you realling going to breed from it? Is it for the status or are you really going in for field trials? If not, do not be too choosy since you are less likely to buy a disaster who only reveals his eccentricities in the middle of the best drive of the season after a couple of perfect seasons.

Labrador

For elegance, reliability and general-purposefulness, a Labrador has no peer, although a Retriever runs it fairly close. The main qualities of a Labrador are: friendliness, loyalty, athleticism, ease to train, strength, hardiness, stamina, adaptability, steadiness, intelligence, trustworthiness with children and a desire to please. Conversely, a Labrador is fairly large, more circumspect about diving into just any piece of cover, often a scavenger in the vein of Attila the Hun, and less likely to work flat out all day on a rough shoot without a noticeable tailing off in performance.

Spaniel

By and large, shooting men in Great Britain either have Labradors or Spaniels. The debate over their relative merits is steeped in the mists of time and is never likely to diminish in its intensity. Spaniels' good qualities are: an ability to work flat out all day without respite, boundless energy, compactness and therefore better ability to work thick cover, nimbleness, agility and friendliness. Their minus points are, and remember these are generalizations and not necessarily applicable to every single dog: excitability; ability to attract dirt, burrs and foreign bodies, especially in and around their ears; greater resistance to training; and need for greater discipline.

If a gun dog becomes ill-disciplined, it can be redeemed only with difficulty in the case of the Labrador, whereas a Spaniel is almost impossible to bring back to its peak.

Retriever

Retrievers are very similar to Labradors in almost all respects. The only significant difference is that Retrievers have long coats and, like Spaniels, tend to attract every burr and twig within a ten-foot radius of action.

Flatcoat Retriever

Flatcoats are black and long-coated. While they have most of the characteristics of Labradors and Retrievers, they tend to be more excitable and challenging to control. By way of categorization, Flatcoats fall somewhere between Labradors and Spaniels in temperament. They are usually brilliant in water.

Pointer and Setter

Both breeds are not really suited to driven shooting. Prospective buyers are advised to seek guidance and advice, possibly from the National Gundog Association. Both breeds tend to be fairly highly-strung, Pointers being more wary of strangers and less predictable in their behaviour, whereas Setters are very friendly (and sloppy).

Dog or Bitch?

Some people say that bitches are more placid, more steady and more loyal than dogs. This is an erroneous generalization since the key lies with the owner and how he or she handles the animal.

In the simplest terms, bitches come into season twice a year, of which once will always coincide with the shooting season. Since it is very bad form to take a bitch in season shooting – because it completely destroys the concentration of all male dogs present – this means being without a dog for at least two weeks. Of course a bitch can be spayed, a process that can render – but not always – a bitch permanently 'interesting' to other dogs. This is unfortunate since the innocent owner will have to suffer thinly veiled sneers as much as if his bitch really was in season: 'It's damned irresponsibile to bring a bitch in season, etc. etc . . .'

A good bitch can be a lucrative source of income in terms of breeding potential, though; but, if choosing a gun-dog, this should not be a first priority.

Dogs do not suffer from the same problems but may be less steady. Once indoctrinated in the ways of the birds and bees, there is a danger that they will try to roam. They can earn money through stud fees. Although the income will only equate to the cost of one pup from the resultant litter, there is not the attendant inconvenience of raising and selling a whole litter.

Breeding Etiquette

It is worth mentioning a few points of etiquette concerning the breeding of dogs. It is customary to take the bitch to the dog, since it is the bitch owner's responsibility to seek a mate. One advantage of so doing is that the dog is less likely to develop a roaming instinct; the theory being that he will not think he has to travel in search of satisfaction. The dog owner's payment is either the same as the selling price of one pup or pick of the litter. Litters from two pedigree, Kennel Club-registered dogs should be registered immediately; this makes the pups more valuable which, in turn, will apply to their progeny.

Whatever the choice of breed and sex, a dog is only as good as its master. If a dog does not work for you, it is unlikely that any other dog will either; miracles are not common in this sphere. True, a poor or even rogue animal could be the cause, but real rogues are relatively rare. Whatever the case, before condemning a dog as useless, ask an expert to try their hand with it first.

Care of Dogs When Shooting

So many owners, the author being no exception, tend to take their dogs for granted. The points that follow may go some way towards redressing the situation.

Equipment

Regardless of the weather forecast, always assume the worst will happen and that, even if it does not rain, your dog will find some way of drenching itself, usually towards the end of the last drive. With this criterion in mind, you should be able to plan your dog's needs by covering every eventuality at little inconvenience to yourself and considerable benefit to your dog. Items to include are:

Lead
Whistle
Tether – if necessary
Bed – if a long journey is entailed
Towelling bag, or at least a towel
Snack for lunch – a few biscuits
Evening meal – if a long journey is entailed

Dog bowl – in the event of a meal being necessary
Water
Water bowl
First Aid Kit – see Chapter Six

What a Dog Might Expect From His Master During The Day

A dog's demands are extraordinarily unonerous, especially when one considers what the dog does in return. From a dog's point of view, it would be reasonable to expect his master to do the following, as the day progresses:

Provide breakfast if there will be a lot of work to do, assuming that the dog does not usually have breakfast.

Remember to load all his kit (the dog's) in the car.

Not let the dog attempt anything foolish, such as jumping high barbed wire fences, and not letting him over-extend himself.

Inspect for thorns and injuries at lunch.

Provide a few biscuits and water if there has been none available previously.

Inspect for thorns, etc. before going home.

If wet, either put into a towelling bag or rub with a towel. Dogs are just as prone as humans to the vagaries of rheumatism and arthritis.

If a long journey means a late return, the dog should be fed, otherwise feed on return home.

A thorough check for thorns and injuries.

n.b. This rather presupposes that most owners feed their dogs their main meal in the evenings which, obviously, is not always the case. It is important not to disrupt the dog's feeding pattern.

8
TREATMENT OF GAME

Having shot one's quarry it is necessary to know how to dispatch it, carry it, hang it and prepare it for the table. Often the hunter's responsibilities stop there. Thus this chapter makes no mention of cooking.

Dispatch

Always dispatch wounded game as soon as possible, with the minimum of suffering. With practice, a sharp knock on the back of the head is the quickest and most effective method, irrespective of species.

Feathered Game

With feathered game either: hold the bird firmly in both hands with the breast uppermost and strike its head hard against a hard surface such as a tree, stone or fence post (only ever use the stock of a gun in desperation and then with the stock flat on the ground, immediately removing any blood from the gun, particularly the metalwork) or hold the bird by the neck in one hand and strike the back of its head firmly with a stick, taking care not to kill your fingers. To test whether the bird, and indeed any species, is dead or not, breathe on or touch an eye, which should appear dull and glazed but, more obviously, should not blink if the creature is dead.

It is possible, as another alternative, with young grouse and smaller species (partridge, snipe, woodcock), to kill them by crushing their skulls. The technique is to hold the bird by the neck between forefinger and second finger, and squeeze down with your thumb on the top of the skull until you feel it break inwards. This is a rapid and easy means of dispatch but, if inexperienced, do avoid protracting the process.

With practice it is possible to kill a pheasant by a deft and not over-exuberant twist of the neck. This is not suitable for other species, particularly grouse, partridge and pigeon, since the head is apt to part company with the body with astonishing ease. On the other hand, it is wellnigh impossible to wring the neck of a duck or a goose, both of which have necks of inordinate elasticity, and it should not be attempted. Quite apart from the suffering that will be caused, the birds are likely to be grossly disfigured. Another method is to use a Priest, which is a short (6") cosh, normally used by fishermen. If there is still room in your pockets, then it might be a most useful device.

If lucky enough to pick a snipe or woodcock, remove the legs beneath the 'knees' immediately, while still warm and before rigor mortis renders the operation much harder and probably impossible. The technique is to hold the thigh firmly between forefinger and thumb, hold the lower limb, break it and pull firmly. After some resistance the lower leg will come away along with the tendons, which are like slivers of bone if left for cooking. The result of this action will be that each thigh can be eaten whole less the single thigh bone in the middle; otherwise, woodcock and snipe legs are hardly worth the effort since they are so boney or, more accurately, sinewy.

Ground Game

Rabbits and hares may be dispatched identically. While they too can be killed by a sharp knock on the head as described, this method is neither necessary nor recommended. Take either species by both hind legs, holding upsidedown firmly in your non-master hand. With the master hand administer a sharp, downwards, karate-style chop to the back of the neck. You will only hurt your hand if you fail to use sufficient determination in what is a surprisingly simple procedure. Hares, when wounded, scream in the most heart-rending, pathetic fashion; do not be deterred but, rather, use this as an incentive to dispatch the beast as quickly as possible. Once either species is dead, hold the animal tail downwards in both hands, squeezing progressively on the abdomen to evacuate the bladder, which will otherwise do so where you would prefer it did not.

Rabbits should be paunched (gutted) on arrival at home.

Many people do the same with hares, although others prefer them hung intact for a few days. If you are rash enough to shoot a hare a long way from home on a rough or walked-up shoot, it is customary to carry it yourself. Since hares are horribly weighty, it is quite acceptable to gut them on the spot to lighten the load, although this should not be necessary on a driven shoot.

Some Do's and Don'ts

Don't shoot wounded quarry except for strongly running hares and rabbits and then only if it is safe to do so. Apart from the fact that it is very dangerous to shoot at close quarters, particularly due to the risk from ricochets, the quarry is likely to be destroyed or rendered useless for eating.

Do make every reasonable effort to find wounded game but temper this with common sense, and **don't** delay the next drive too long lest you disrupt the whole day's programme, for which your host will certainly not thank you.

Do try to get a dog to seek out wounded game but **don't** let it, or indeed yourself, chase a runner into the next drive's covert since it will most certainly ruin that drive by disturbing the game in it. If in doubt, check with the keeper before sending your dog in.

Carriage of Game

In principle, game should be carried the same way up that it will be hung at home. Thus feathered game should be carried by the neck, head uppermost, while rabbits and hares should be carried by the hind legs, head at the bottom. (At times, on the continent, some smaller game birds are hung by the feet). With rabbits and hares, convenience dictates the method of carriage as much as anything else . . . if in doubt, try carrying them head uppermost.

For the journey home from a shoot, there is no harm in placing game on its side, although for a journey of several hours in a probably warm car, game should be hung. Unless you trust your dog implicitly, it is as well not to put your game where the dog can feast himself; nor is it fair to do so.

Hanging Game

Without going into a biological dissertation as to why game should hang and not lie on its side, suffice it to say that game on its side decomposes beyond the edible very quickly; usually overnight.

With most species, hanging positively improves the flavour. If you think chicken is bland, it is exquisite compared to a pheasant that has not been hung at all. Some people maintain that hanging makes old birds less tough. While there may be some truth in this, in reality this theory is only true if the bird is hung to the point of decomposition; it is the method of cooking that is critical.

It is most convenient to hang birds in pairs. Simply tie a noose of string with a slip knot around one bird and do the same with the other end of the string round the second bird. Then hang them over a nail or hook. With rabbits and hares, cut a slit in one hind leg, right through between the bone and tendon above the bottom joint, force the other leg through the slit and then hang over a hook.

Hang game unplucked with stomach intact, in a cool, well-ventilated, shaded place protected from predators such as pets and especially cats. A garage is often the nearest solution available but should be made cat-proof, i.e. keep the doors closed. Everybody has their own ideas on length of hanging; in essence, it depends very much on the weather, on the species, and on personal taste. If the body comes away from the head, it may be safe to say that the game is overhung! The following times are fairly conservative since the author prefers his game to be not too gamey:

Species	Minimum	Maximum
Grouse	1 day	7 days
Ptarmigan	,,	,,
Partridge	2/3 days	,,
Pheasant	4 days	10/12 days
Duck	1 day	5/6 days
Woodcock	,,	3 days
Snipe	,,	,,
Pigeon	,,	,,
Hare	4 days	10 days
Rabbit	1 day	3 days

n.b. In very mild weather, these times could be halved.

Plucking

The longer they hang, the harder birds are to pluck without tearing the skin. There are many ways to pluck a bird and only experience can really provide the best method. To some extent, it is true to say that the larger the bird, the harder it is to pluck. Incidentally, the same principles apply to all birds except pigeons. Pigeons differ in that, while they can be treated as any other species, it is equally simple to pluck the breasts, and then cut them off, discarding the rest, including the skin from each breast.

Herewith 2 methods of plucking:

1. Fill a sink with warm water, have a plastic carrier bag to hand and a pair of good quality game shears/scissors; failing the shears, a robust, sharp knife will suffice. Remove the legs immediately above the knee, leaving the thigh intact. Remove the wings at the first joint of the wing. Removal of these extremities makes the bird more manageable and saves unnecessary plucking.

Now work to a sequence. For example, pluck the tail feathers first, then the legs, then the back, finishing with the front or underside, which is the most fiddly bit and where the skin is most likely to rip. To reduce the risk of tearing the skin, take a few feathers at a time between finger and thumb, as near their base as possible, holding the bird on the draining board firmly in the other hand with its head furthest away from you. Jerk the feathers quickly in the direction of the head, putting the feathers in the water. Try to get into the habit of pressing against the flesh around the area being plucked at the same time as plucking or else you will tear the skin very easily.

Once you reach the neck, pluck just enough feathers so that when you decapitate the bird you do not remove any breast. Cut off the head and neck as near the breast as possible and discard. With grouse, pheasants, geese, duck and partridges, press gently on the centre of the breast bone to evacuate the crop of its contents – recently fed pheasants' crops will contain corn while grouse's will contain heather. Turn the bird round and make an inch-long incision in the underside of the anus with the shears. Insert two fingers and remove the innards before rinsing through under cold water. The squeamish may prefer to don rubber gloves prior to this last operation. Please note that woodcock, quail and snipe are not worth gutting and are best cooked with their innards *in situ*. With a pheasant, this whole process will take anything between ten and thirty minutes depending on experience.

Put all the feathers, extremities and gory bits in the carrier bag and throw in the dustbin. Responsibility for the bird may then be entrusted to the cook.

It is worth singling out duck. Duck have a mass of fluffy down, close to their skin, which is a nuisance to pluck perfectly. When you have tired of removing the down and are left with a few wisps, lightly singe them with a naked flame without burning the flesh.

2. The following method really only applies to geese, mallard or pheasants, everything else being small enough to comfortably hold in one hand. Hold the bird firmly and pluck the feathers from both sides of the wings, close to the body, before cutting off the two outer sections of the wings.

Tie the bird's feet together and hang on a convenient nail or hook over a sack or dustbin, inside an outhouse or garage; feathers will blow all over the place outside. Also, unless your outhouse is heated, this method, late in the season, is recommended only for the hardiest sportsman.

Pluck downwards, towards the head, using the same plucking technique as the first method described. Once plucked, remove the legs and head and gut as before.

Skinning

The process of skinning and gutting hares and rabbits is more or less identical for each species.

Lay the animal on its back. Make a shallow incision with a sharp knife between the forelegs and continue the cut down to the hind legs. The cut should be shallow enough to cut the skin but not penetrate into the stomach. Grip the skin either side of the incision and gently pull apart to expose the stomach. Turn the animal over. Hold the head and hind legs and very sharply flick the body down, which should eject the stomach. Cut the connections at either end, releasing the stomach, and then remove any other internal organs which may still be attached.

Remove the feet, then gently prise the skin from around the body as much as possible so that only the head and legs are covered. Bend the body backwards to enable the hind legs to be pulled out of the skin, possibly applying the knife around the tail. Pull the skin towards the head, over the forelegs, thus leaving the skin attached to the head. Cut off the head, close to the shoulders. Once again, the point has been reached where the cook assumes command.

9
THE LAW

The details in this chapter reflect the changes in the Firearms and Shot Gun laws brought about by the Firearms (Amendments) Act 1988, which came into force on the first of July 1989. The material is quoted verbatim from the Home Office publications listed below and must not be reproduced in whole or in part without permission from the Home Office:

Firearms – Changes In The Firearms Law, HMSO pub. Dd8950284 HOME J0849 NJ, dated November 1988.

Firearms – A Guide To The Law, HMSO pub. Dd8172002 HOME J1043 NJ, dated May 1989.

Firearms – Gun Permits For Visitors To Great Britain, HMSO pub. Dd8170300 HOME J1044 NJ.

Licences

Game licence. It is an offence to take or kill game (defined as: Blackgame, Deer, Grouse, Hare, Partridge, Pheasant, Rabbit – if taken unlawfully, Snipe and Woodcock) if not in possession of a Game Licence. Exemptions include: Farmers, or persons authorised by them, when shooting hare and rabbit. There are several types of Game Licence available, from Post Offices, as follows:

Red Game Licence – Valid for 1 year, 1 August–31 July.

Green Game Licence – Valid from 1 August–31 October.

Blue Game Licence – Valid from 1 November–31 July.

Occasional Licence – Valid for 14 days.

The Purchase, Possession and Use of Shot Guns By Juniors

Under 15
It is an offence to make a gift of a shot gun or ammunition to a

person under 15 years old. A person may not have an assembled shot gun with him except:

when he is under the direct supervision of someone of or over 21, in which case, providing he has a valid shot gun certificate, he may use the shot gun under that person's instruction, or

when the shot gun is in a securely fastened gun cover so that it cannot be fired.

Age 15 to 17

A person between the ages of 15 and 17 may be given or lent a shot gun and ammunition but he may not buy them.

After reaching the age of 15, a person may use a shot gun without supervision, providing he holds a valid shot gun certificate.

Age 17

On reaching the age of 17, a person may purchase a shot gun providing he holds a valid shot gun certificate, and he may buy ammunition also.

Changes In The Firearms Law As A Result Of The Firearms (Amendment) Act 1988

Prohibited Weapons

These weapons are now prohibited (in addition to those prohibited by Section 5 of The Firearms Act 1968):

Burst fire weapons. These are firearms which can fire two or more missiles successively without repeated pressure on the trigger.

Self-loading rifles and carbines except those chambered for .22 rim-fire cartridges.

Pump-action rifles and carbines except those chambered for .22 rim-fire cartridges.

Self-loading smooth-bore guns with barrels shorter than 24″ or an overall length of 40″, except those chambered for .22 rim-fire cartridges. Folding or detachable butt-stocks are discounted when establishing length.

Pump-action smooth-bore guns with barrels shorter than 24″ or an overall length of 40″, except those chambered for .22 rimfire cartridges (see above for stocks).

Smooth-bore revolver guns except muzzle-loading guns and those chambered for 9 mm rim-fire cartridges.

Rocket launchers and mortars except launchers for fireworks, signal flares and safety lines.

Any of the above weapons, or any fully automatic weapon converted to a lower category (see Converted Weapons).

Prohibited weapons may be lawfully possessed, purchased, acquired, manufactured, sold or transferred only with the authority of The Secretary of State. Authority is not normally given to permit possession by private individuals.

Weapons That Need A Firearm Certificate

Certain weapons which previously could be held on a shot gun certificate have been reclassified and in future will be subject to control under Section 1 of The Firearms Act 1968. Readers wanting advice on the possession of rifles, pistols and Section 1 ammunition, should contact their local police; these details are not included here because they are not directly relevant to game shooting. So if you already own, or wish to possess, purchase or acquire one of these guns, you will need to obtain a firearm certificate from your local police. A certificate will not be issued unless the police are satisfied that you have shown a good reason for possessing the gun, and that you may be trusted to possess it without danger to public safety or the peace.

The weapons which have been reclassified and which now need a firearm certificate are:

any smooth-bore gun with a bore of more than 2″ in diameter or a barrel less than 24″ in length.

any smooth-bore gun with a detachable magazine or magazine that can hold more than two cartridges.

smooth-bore revolver guns, chambered for 9 mm rim-fire cartridges or muzzle-loading.

Estate rifles. There are circumstances when a firearm certificate is not needed to possess a rifle and ammunition. A person aged 17 or over may borrow a rifle from the occupier of private premises and use it only in his (or his employee's) presence on those premises, that:

a firearm certificate for the rifle is held by the occupier of the premises or his employee, and the person who borrows and uses the rifle complies with the conditions on the relevant certificate.

Anyone using a rifle in these circumstances may also acquire or buy ammunition during the period of the loan up to the maximum amount allowed by the relevant certificate.

Weapons That Need A Shot Gun Certificate

A shot gun certificate is needed to permit the lawful possession, purchase or acquisition of a smooth-bore gun under Section 2 of The Firearms Act 1968 (certain smooth-bore guns need a firearm certificate or Section 5 authority – see Prohibited Weapons and Weapons That Need A Firearm Certificate, previously). This is a smooth-bore gun which has a barrel length of 24″ or more, and a bore of 2″ or less, provided that:

it is not a revolver gun and

it has either no magazine or has a non-detachable magazine which can hold no more than two cartridges.

If the gun has a magazine which has been adapted to hold no more than two cartridges, then the gun must be certified as such by a Proof House unless constructed from new in this way.

The police may refuse to issue a shot gun certificate if they are satisfied that an applicant does not have a good reason for possessing the gun, or cannot be permitted to possess a shotgun without danger to public safety or the peace.

A shot gun certificate will specify the description of the shotguns to which it relates. This will include, where known, the identification numbers of the guns. Under the new Firearms Rules, shotgun owners also need to satisfy the police as to the security of weapons when not in use, and to inform them immediately of any theft and change of permanent address.

The transfer of a shotgun to anyone who is not a registered firearms dealer must be notified to the local police within seven days of the transfer. Both the person who transfers the gun and the person who receives it must notify their local police. 'Transfer' includes loans of longer than 72 hours and the sale, hire or gift of a gun.

Purchase of Ammunition

If you buy ammunition (except ammunition that is subject to control under Sections 1 or 5 of The Firearms Act 1968), you must produce the appropriate firearms or shotgun certificate; or written authority from a certificate holder, authorizing you to buy it, together with the holder's original certificate.

This requirement does not apply if you sell ammunition as part of your business.

Common Expiry Dates Of Firearms And Shotgun Certificates

From 1 July 1989, firearm and shot gun certificates may be issued to have a common expiry date. If you already hold both such certificates, you may be able to renew your shot gun certificate at a reduced cost when either of them runs out.

Converted Weapons

If a prohibited weapon has been converted to bring it under a different category of control, it will still remain a prohibited weapon. The conversion makes no difference to this.

If a weapon has at any time been subject to control under Section 1 of the Firearms Act 1968, and it has had a rifled barrel of less than 24″, it will keep its classification as a weapon requiring a firearm certificate unless deactivated. The fact that it has been converted to a shot gun or an air weapon does not affect its classification. This also applies to weapons of the type set out under: Weapons That Need A Firearm Certificate.

Other conversions which change the classification are permitted: a bolt-action rifle which had a barrel length of more than 24″ and has since been smooth-bored, and either has no magazine or an integral or fixed magazine which can hold no more than two cartridges, will require a shot gun certificate. If the magazine has been adapted to hold no more than two cartridges, the gun must be certified as such by a Proof House.

Deactivated Weapons

A special scheme has been introduced to exempt weapons of all categories, which have certified as deactivated, from the certification requirements of the Firearms Act. A weapon will be deemed as having been made incapable of discharging any shot, bullet or other missile, if it is marked as deactivated following inspection by a Proof House and the Proof House has issued a certificate of deactivation for the gun.

Gunsmiths can carry out the work needed to deactivate the gun to Government specifications. The gun must then be sent to a Proof House for inspection. If the gun meets the specifications, the Proof House will stamp it with approved marks and certify that the necessary work has been done. The gun will then no longer need certification by the police. An administrative fee will be charged by the Proof House.

Dealers

To be registered as a firearms dealer you must satisfy the police that you are or will engage in business as a firearms dealer to a substantial extent, or as an essential part of another trade or profession. You must maintain a register of all transactions for at least five years for inspection.

Shot Guns – A Guide To The Law

What Is A Shot Gun?

A shot gun is a smooth-bored gun which meets all the following criteria:

has a barrel length of not less than 24″, and a bore of 2″ or less in diameter;

does not have a magazine, or has a non-detachable magazine which cannot hold more than two cartridges; and

is not a revolver gun (i.e. a gun containing a series of chambers which revolve when the gun is fired).

Applying For A Shot Gun Certificate

All shot gun certificates issued on or after 1 July 1989 will be on a form bearing a photograph of the holder.

The certificates will also contain a detailed description of all guns held on the certificate, including any identification numbers if known. You will therefore need to provide this information on the new shot gun certificate application form. A new safekeeping condition will appear on all shot gun certificates. This creates two distinct levels of security to ensure safe custody of the guns.

Criteria For The Issue Of A Shot Gun Certificate

A chief officer of police will not be able to grant a shot gun certificate if:

he is not satisfied that the applicant can possess a shot gun without danger to the public safety or to the peace,

he is satisfied that the applicant does not have good reason for possessing, purchasing or acquiring a gun (examples of good reasons are: sporting or competition purposes, the shooting of vermin, and some situations where the gun is not intended for use, such as if it is an heirloom or part of a collection).

he has reason to believe the applicant is prohibited from possessing a shot gun.

Common Expiry Dates For Shot Gun and Firearm Certificates

A firearm certificate holder applying for the grant or renewal of a shot gun certificate can ask for it to be issued with the same expiry date as his firearm certificate. Alternatively, where a shot gun certificate holder applies for the grant or renewal of a firearm certificate, he may surrender his current shot gun certificate and apply for a new one to take effect on the same day as the firearm certificate. In the latter case, a reduced fee will be paid for the shot gun certificate.

Transfer and Sale of Shot Guns

'Transfer' means sale, letting on hire, giving as a gift or lending for a period of more than 72 hours. These do not apply where the person acquiring the gun is a registered firearms dealer, or someone exempt from the need to hold a certificate.

When both parties to the transfer hold certificates issued or renewed on or after 1 July 1989 (i.e. new-style certificates), the following requirements apply:

A person transferring a shot gun must enter details of the gun on to the new holder's certificate. Within seven days of the transaction he must also send a notice of the transaction to the chief officer of police who issued his shot gun certificate. If the person transferring the shotgun is exempt from the need to hold a certificate, he should notify details of the transaction to the chief officer of police who issued the certificate of the gun's new holder.

A person who acquires a shotgun must send a note of the transaction within seven days of the transaction taking place to chief officer of police who issued his certificate.

The notice sent to the chief officer of police must contain a description of the shotgun (including any identification number) and the nature of any transaction and the name and address of the other person involved in the transaction. This notice must be sent either by Registered Post or Recorded Delivery. A fax is not strictly acceptable.

When one or other or both of the parties involved hold a certificate issued or renewed on or before 30 June 1989, the following requirements apply during the period of validity of the old-style certificate:

If both the person transferring and the person acquiring the shotgun have certificates issued on or before 30 June 1989 (i.e. an old-style certificate), neither need comply with any of the new notification requirements.

If the person transferring the gun holds a certificate issued or renewed on or before 30 June 1989, but the person acquiring the gun holds a new-style certificate, the person transferring the gun must enter the details of the gun on the new holder's certificate. The new holder of the gun must send notice of the transaction to his chief officer of police within seven days.

If the person acquiring the gun holds a certificate issued on or before 30 June 1989 and the person transferring the gun holds a certificate issued on or after 1 July 1989, the person transferring the gun should send a notice of the transaction to his chief officer of police, but the person receiving the gun need not notify his chief officer of police.

Purchase Of Shot Gun Ammunition

You must produce your shot gun certificate when purchasing shotgun ammunition, unless you are exempt from the need to hold a certificate. If, because of the new controls, your gun is classified as a firearm, you will need to produce your firearm certificate.

Penalties

The penalty for possession of a firearm without an appropriate authority is six months imprisonment or a fine of up to £2000.

If you are in any doubt about the status of your gun, you would be wise to contact your local gunsmith or police firearms department. If you are a visitor to Great Britain this section does not apply to you; the following one does, though.

Visitors to Great Britain

From 1 October 1989, visitors wishing to bring a shot gun or firearm into Great Britain, to possess one here, or to purchase a shot gun for personal use here, will need to obtain a visitor's firearm or shot gun permit.

Who Needs A Visitor's Permit?

You will need a permit if you are not resident in Great Britain and wish to:

bring a firearm or shot gun into Great Britain for use on a private estate for sport, or to take part in a shooting competition or event.

buy a shot gun in Great Britain for use here, or to take home with you.

use a shot gun which you own in Great Britain, and have lodged here with a registered firearms dealer.

You will not need a permit if you intend to:

purchase a firearm or shot gun for the purpose of exporting it without taking possession of it in Great Britain, provided you have not been in the country for more than 30 days in the preceding twelve months or

borrow a shot gun from the occupier of private premises and use it on those premises in the occupier's presence, or use a shot gun at a time and place approved for shooting at artificial targets by the chief officer of police for the area in which that place is situated, or

borrow a rifle from the occupier of private premises and use it on those premises in either the occupier's presence or that of his employee.

What Permits Entitle the Holder To Do
Visitor's Firearm Permit. If you hold one of these, you may possess the firearm(s) specified on your permit. You may also purchase (on production of your permit), acquire or possess the amount of ammunition specified on the permit.

Visitor's Shot Gun Permit. This entitles you to possess, purchase or acquire the shot gun(s) specified on your permit. You may also purchase (on production of your permit), acquire or possess shot gun ammunition.

What the Permits Cover
A Shot Gun Permit will include details of the number of guns to which it relates, including their description and identification numbers, where known.

A Firearm Permit will include similar details, plus the amount of ammunition you may purchase, possess or acquire, and the maximum amount you may possess at any one time.

Both types of permit will normally include a number of conditions attached by the chief officer of police. These are designed to ensure the safe custody of the weapons and ammunition. These will normally require you to sign the permit on receipt; to report at once to the chief officer of police who issued the permit the theft or loss of any gun or ammunition covered by the permit, and to notify him of any alteration in your arrangements, e.g. any change of address in Great Britain. There will normally be a further condition relating to the safe keeping of the shotgun, firearm or ammunition to which the permit relates.

A Firearm Permit may also contain further conditions relating to where the firearm may be used.

A Shot Gun Permit which has been issued in order to allow you to purchase a shot gun in Great Britain will normally have a condition requiring you to notify the police of the purchase of the shot gun and to enter details of the shot gun on the face of the permit.

The Period of Validity of your permit (which may be up to a maximum of twelve months from the date of issue) will be indicated on the face of the permit.

How to Apply For a Permit
An application for either type of permit will need to be made on your behalf by a sponsor, resident in Great Britain, to the chief officer of police for the area in which the sponsor lives. Application forms are available from local police stations. The sponsor may be a private individual or a representative of a club, shooting syndicate, country estate or a national shooting organisation; he need not necessarily hold a firearm or shotgun certificate himself.

The **sponsor** should complete the application form on your behalf. He will need to give details of all the places you intend to shoot and events you intend to participate in, and deal with any queries from the police, and will forward the permit to you once it has been issued.

As the **visitor**, you will need to supply the sponsor with details (including serial numbers) of the shot gun(s) or firearm(s) you wish to use or bring with you, the shot gun(s) you wish to purchase in Great Britain, and the reason for purchasing or possessing them. You may not be able to change the weapons you supplied details for unless you give sufficient notice.

The **chief officer of police** will need to be satisfied that you have a good reason for having the shot gun(s) or firearm(s) and ammunition while visiting Great Britain (or, in the case of a permit issued for the purchase of a shot gun, that you have a good reason for purchasing it); that you do not represent a danger to the public safety or to the peace; and that you are not prohibited from possessing the gun concerned.

The **application** should be made in good time in order to

give the police sufficient time to complete their enquiries; ideally six to eight weeks before you intend to travel to Great Britain. If, once an application has been made, you wish to change your plans – for instance by changing the type or number guns you wish to bring, or by adding or subtracting numbers in a group application – you should let your sponsor know as soon as possible so that he can advise the police. The police will make every effort to accommodate such changes but it will not always be possible to do so.

A **group application** may be made by a sponsor for up to 20 permits for visitors specified in the application. In such cases, in addition to the criteria outlined above, the chief officer of police will need to be satisfied that the persons specified in the application intend to use the shot gun(s) or firearm(s) in question, either for sporting purposes on the same private premises during the same period, or to participate in the same competitions or events.

A **fee** is payable, to cover the administrative costs, when a visitor's firearm or shot gun permit is granted. Where 6 or more permits are issued as a group application, this fee is reduced.

If the application is **refused**, the notification of refusal, along with reasons for the decision, will be sent by letter to your sponsor. Every effort will be made to send it in good time to avoid you incurring unnecessary travel costs. There is **no** right of appeal against the refusal.

If, once you have been issued with a permit and have arrived in Great Britain, you decide to compete in some event or other events, you may make a verbal or written request for a variation (on a new application form) to the chief officer of police who issued your permit. If the event is to take place after the expiry date of the existing permit, it will be necessary for a fresh application to be made for a new permit. This should be made in writing on a new application form by the sponsor of the new event to his chief of local police.

When to Have Your Permit Available

You should show your permit to the Customs Officer at your port of entry into Great Britain. Failure to do so may render your gun(s) liable to detention or seizure.

You should retain your permit until you leave the country, as you may be required to present it to a Customs Officer at your port of embarkation. You may also wish to keep the permit for future use if it has not expired. If you do not wish to keep the permit, you should return it to the chief officer of police who issued it.

Further Information

If you are not sure whether you require a visitor's permit, or if you would like further advice on this subject, you should contact your local British Embassy, High Commission or other representative of Her Majesty's Government. Alternatively, you may ask your prospective sponsor to contact his local police. If you are thinking of sponsoring a visitor to Great Britain and require further guidance, you should contact the BASC first and then your local police.

Visitors to Great Britain should read the Home Office leaflet: 'Gun Permits for Visitors to Great Britain', available from Police Stations and: HMSO Publications, PO Box 276, London SW8 5DT (Tel.: Orders–071 873 9090, Enquiries–071 873 0011).

10
SHOOTING AGENTS

Shooting Within The British Isles

Shooting agents let various forms of shooting in a variety of ways. Days can be bought singly by individuals or by groups for one or more days. Shooting agents do not usually find places for individuals wishing to join a syndicate on a permanent basis, although it may be worth asking. Membership of a syndicate is usually through advertisements in shooting periodicals or by word of mouth.

Agents advertise regularly in all the country and shooting-oriented magazines. In addition, many of the top estate agents maintain departments specializing in the letting of shooting.

Shooting Abroad

These days there are wonderful opportunities to shoot abroad, whether it is partridge in Spain, pheasants in Hungary (beware, since some of the shooting is very commercialized and not very sporting), quail in Florida or duck and geese in Canada.

There are agents who specialize in organising these events which is just as well since shooting abroad can be fraught with pitfalls. Each country has its own laws with regard to such details as: the movement of firearms into and out of the destination country; game licences; shotgun and firearm certificate requirements and the carriage and purchase of ammunition – for example, India allows only 50 cartridges to be brought in by one person and Indian-made ammunition is expensive and different in quality to that available at home.

It is not practicable to tabulate the legal requirements that must be satisfied for other countries since changes occur so frequently. Anyone wishing to shoot abroad should use the services and expertise of a shooting agent. Those confident enough to organise their own trips are still advised to seek advice from the relevant embassy or consulate. Even then, it is advisable to seek further information from a helpful agent who might be aware of problems that will not necessarily be mentioned by the embassy staff.

11
GAMESHOOTING SEASONS

Seasons when different game species can be shot vary, even within the British Isles. The tables below cover England, Scotland, Wales, Northern Ireland (NI) and, although not part of the United Kingdom but for convenience's sake, Eire (E).

Species	Season (all dates inclusive)	Shot Size (recommended)	Comment
Birds			
Blackgame	20 Aug.–10 Dec.	6 or 7	
Capercailzie	1 Oct.–31 Jan.	3, 4 or 5	
Duck/Goose	1 Sept.–31 Jan.	4, 5 or 6	Inland
	1 Sept.–20 Feb.	(Goose:	Foreshore
		1 or 3)	
	(NI: 1 Sept.–31 Jan.)		
	(E: 1 Sept.–31 Jan.)		
Grouse	12 Aug.–10 Dec.	6 or 7	
	(NI: 12 Aug.–30 Nov.)		
	(E: 12 Aug.–30 Sept.)		Cork, Kerry, Mayo
	1 Sept.–30 Sept.		All other areas
Partridge	1 Sept.–1 Feb.	6 or 7	
	(NI: 1 Oct.–31 Jan.)		
	(E: 1 Nov.–15 Nov.)		
Pheasant	1 Oct.–1 Feb.	5, 6 or 7	Most shoots wait until end Oct. or 1 Nov.
	(NI: 1 Oct.–31 Jan.)		
	(E: 1 Nov.–31 Jan.)		
Ptarmigan	12 Aug.–10 Dec.	6 or 7	
Snipe	12 Aug.–31 Jan.	7 or 8	
	(NI: 1 Sept.–31 Jan.)		
	(E: – ,, –)		

Woodcock	1 Oct.–31 Jan.	6 or 7	England and Wales
	1 Sept.–31 Jan.		Scotland
	(E: – „ –)		
Pigeon	Any Time	6 or 7	

Mammals

Hare	All year	4 or 5	
	(NI: 1 Feb.–11 Aug.)		
	(E: 26 Sept.–28 Feb.)		
Rabbit	All year	5 or 6	

Shot Size Equivalents

English	American Swedish	French	Belgian	Italian	Spanish
1	2	3	–	1 or 2	3
3	4	4	–	3	4
4	5	5	–	4	5
5	6	6	5	5	6
6	–	–	6	6	–
7	7½	7	7	7½	7
7½	8	7½	7½	8	7½
8	–	8	8	–	8
9	9	9	9	9½	9

APPENDIX 1: GLOSSARY

There is little more discomfiting for a novice who is trying to conceal that fact, than hearing his peers using incomprehensible terms. Equally, the sensible novice refrains from over-use of jargon if he is not to stand out as a novice. He should let on that he is a beginner, on the basis that such an admission should result in people offering help and advice; it also warns them to be wary of the actions of a novice. To pretend to be experienced when the opposite is the case is to invite ridicule at best and disgrace in the event of a mistake.

The following list is not all-embracing, but should go a long way towards helping the novice to understand what people are talking about in the shooting field.

The Action Contains the gun's firing mechanism; joins the stock to the barrels.

Automatic A repeating shotgun which can fire anything up to eight cartridges before reloading. See Chapter Nine for the legal implications of owning an automatic. While useful for vermin and pest control, automatics should not be used for gameshooting other than rough shooting.

Bag The total number of birds and ground game shot during the day.

Balled Shot When pellets fuse to make one shot. Rare and almost invariably destroys the target. Often used as an excuse (a threadbare one) by greedy shots who have destroyed a bird too close to the end of their barrels.

Beater A person who beats the undergrowth as part of the process of driving game towards the guns. May be hired, sometimes friends and/or family, sometimes local enthusiasts and frequently a combination of all three.

Bend The distance between the uppermost edge of the shotgun stock (the comb) and the continuation of a line from the muzzle to the breech of a gun.

Blacking/Blueing The blue coloration applied to protect gun barrels and, to an extent, reduce shine. Sometimes actions are blued too, especially those of guns made abroad.

Bore (or Gauge) In simple terms, the nominal internal diameter of a gun barrel. Occasionally, you may hear the phrase 'checking the bore' which means checking inside the barrels for obstructions. Also a person who bangs on interminably about shooting to the exclusion of anything else.

Box-Lock A simple, robust action; often recognizeable by its squared appearance where it joins the stock.

Brace A pair. Grouse bags, for example, are tallied in braces, e.g. 102½ brace is 205 head.

Broken Gun Where the barrels are dropped open and clear of the action, exposing the chambers to view.

Bullet A shaped lead projectile attached to a (usually) brass case containing explosive propellant. Fired from a rifle or handgun.

Butt The rear or shoulder end of the gun's stock. Also, a butt on a grouse moor, which is an open shelter provided for each Gun; its purpose being not so much protection as concealment from the quarry.

Cartridge Rifle, pistol or shotgun ammunition. Never mix different calibres in the same container, e.g. 12 bore and 20 bore, or a smaller cartridge may block the barrel ahead of a larger one and cause the gun to burst.

Cartridge Bag A waterproof leather or canvas bag. The most common type is a capacious container with cutaway, flap and leather/webbing shoulder strap. They are available in 50, 75 and 100-cartridge sizes; 100 cartridges are not light. A good leather one will last more than a lifetime. For shotgun ammunition only.

Cartridge Base The metal base of the cartridge in the centre of which is the primer. When struck by the firing pin, or striker, the primer ignites the main charge of the cartridge, thereby propelling the shot down the barrel. Some modern cartridges are a one-piece plastic moulding with a primer in the base.

Cartridge Belt A looped belt which usually carries 25 cartridges (the standard quantity in a box). The closed loop system is probably the best since it prevents cartridges slipping through, as can occur with open loops.

Cast The gentle bend in the stock from the centre line of the barrels to allow for vagaries of eyesight and physique. Cast-off is to the right, the cast-on is to the left.

Chamber Where the cartridge is placed in the barrel prior to firing. Make sure your cartridges can be used safely in your gun's chambers. Chamber length and service pressure is usually marked on English proved guns.

Choke The degree of narrowing of the bore at the muzzle end of the barrel. Most shotguns have little or no choke in the right barrel and a varying amout in the left. The aim is to concentrate the shot into a smaller area, thereby slightly increasing the effective range.

Cocks-Only Day A day when you do not shoot hen pheasants. A practice usually confined to post-Christmas days and not necessarily on all shoots. Hosts will brief.

Covert A plantation or small wood offering shelter to birds. The 't' is silent.

Covey A family of grouse or partridge flying together – usually low and very fast. A very large group of several coveys is known as a pack.

Damascus Barrels A nineteenth-century method used to make the best shotgun barrels, now superseded. Damascus barrels may be recognised by the attractive and intricate scrolled patterns which are the result of several pieces of steel being twisted together, fused and drilled.

Decoy An imitation bird which is placed in an advantageous position to lure live birds – either pigeon or duck – over the guns.

Draw On most shoots, Guns draw numbers for their first stand or peg. Thereafter, they move up usually two places each drive. For the draw, most hosts use a pack of cards or purpose-made pegs. Miniatures of whisky or whatever with a number on the bottom is another method seen by the author.

Drive A day will be divided into a number of drives (six or eight average). After each drive, Guns move a pre-arranged number of pegs for the next drive. Most shoots usually number from the right and move two places numerically after each drive.

Driven Game Game driven towards standing Guns by beaters.

Ejector The mechanism on shotguns by which spent cartridge cases are ejected automatically from the gun when it is opened after firing.

Flighting The means by which wildfowl are shot along flight lines, either on inland pools or on coastal marshes and mudflats at dawn or dusk.

Flush To make game break cover and fly over the Guns. A flush can also refer to several birds flushed in a pack; which process keepers try to avoid.

Fouling The deposits left in the barrel after firing which with corrosive caps will cause pitting if not cleaned out immediately after use.

Game Within the meaning of the Game Act 1831, the following quarry species are game: Pheasant, Partridge, Grouse, Ptarmigan, Blackgame, Capercailzie, Snipe, Woodcock, Duck, Goose and Hare.

Game Book In which the sportsman records his adventures: where, with whom, the bag, a brief résumé of the day, and any highlights – you should write only what you do not mind others reading!

Game Cart A trailer or vehicle in which dead game is collected and carried during the day.

Game Dealer A man who sells game – can be a precarious way of earning a living.

Gapes A disease found in pheasants and partridges which affects the throat and is highly infectious.

Ground Game Rabbits and hares. More exotically, also deer, and, on the Continent, such species as mouflon and wild boar.

Gun In addition to the obvious, a term used for a man shooting. 'Game shot' or 'Gameshooter' is a term for a person who indulges in gameshooting.

Gun Case A compartmentalized case, usually of leather-on-wood construction, for transporting and storing a gun. Left in the car while shooting.

Gun Dog Often a misnomer applied by game shots to their spirited pets. In reality, categories are: Setter, Retriever (Labrador, Retriever and Spaniel) and HPRs (Hunter, Pointer, Retrievers). In the USA, Beagles are also used for shooting.

Gun Sleeve (also Gun Cover) A canvas, plastic or leather protective sleeve in which to carry a gun throughout the day. Particularly useful between drives, especially if a fair amount of vehicle travel is involved.

Hammer Gun An obsolescent type of shotgun with outside hammers which usually require manual cocking and rarely have safety catches or ejectors. Not for beginners or serious social shooters but they have their devotees and in practised hands can perform well.

Hanging Feathered game should be hung vertically by the neck for several days, depending on the species and according to personal taste; ground game being hung by the hind legs. This is for culinary reasons rather than some quirky, exotic ritual.

Hide A place of concealment from which to shoot such species as pigeon and wildfowl.

High/Tall Birds Self-explanatory. One of the most sporting targets is a high pheasant with the wind up its tail. The most frequently missed target, a high bird is one at the extreme range (40 yards) of a shotgun.

Hill Something very steep in Scotland, and the somewhat misleading term for a mountain there. Grouse moors in Scotland are often half-way up very steep mountains.

Hip-flask A source of comfort, usually containing an alcoholic beverage according to the owner's taste. Examples are: sloe gin, sloe vodka, cherry brandy, whisky, whisky and Drambuie, whisky and ginger. Try to refrain from producing your flask until after the first drive – it lasts longer that way. A flask is a marvellous ice-breaker and means of introducing yourself to strangers. Shooting and alcohol make very poor bedfellows . . .

Keeper The man without whom you would have no sport, in all likelihood. In the phrase 'Game-keeper', the word 'game' is silent.

Lead Another way of saying forward allowance. The muzzles should be ahead of the target to a varying degree when pulling the trigger. Also an item owners of ill-disciplined dogs always seem to leave at home.

Lock The firing mechanism part of the action. See **Box-lock** and **Side-lock**.

Magazine A leather case with internal compartments, slightly larger than an attaché case, for the carriage of cartridges. An average capacity is about 250 cartridges. Rarely seen except on formal, two-gun days requiring a lot of cartridges.

Mark A word for warning a fellow Gun that a bird is approaching him. An alternative, more usual cry is 'Over'. Such cries are usually only necessary when birds are hard to see or likely to pass unnoticed. They are seldom heard on large, formal shoots. Also the term for marking the fall of a bird for pickers-up.

Over-and-Under (O/U) A two-barrelled shotgun with one barrel over the other.

Pattern The concentration of pellets measured in a circle at a given range (Usually 30 in at 40 yds). .

Peg See **Stand**.

Pellet A small lead ball of which a number make up the shot load, found in a cartridge. A 12 bore cartridge loaded with $1\frac{1}{16}$ oz of No. 6 shot (No. 6) may hold up to 280 pellets.

Picker-up A person, usually with a trained dog, who picks up game, fallen behind the Guns, at the end of the drive. Pickers-up should, depending on the ground, be well back, out of sight and range of the Guns.

Piece Scottish for packed lunch. Also old English for a gun, hence Fowling Piece.

Pitting Corrosion inside barrels due to the effects of rust and fouling in general. Originated by deposits from all cartridges, but especially from cheaper, imported brands. Invariably the result of bad cleaning.

Poking Aiming with the gun already mounted in the shoulder without swinging; which is an excellent way of preserving game since it rarely results in a kill. It is also considered bad form.

Poult An immature pheasant or partridge. Usually released into a temporary pen at 6–8 weeks old.

Priest A small cosh used by fisherman to dispatch fish with. Rarely seen in the shooting field but useful for dispatching birds if room can be found for it in a pocket.

Primer The insert in the centre of the cartridge base which, when struck by the firing pin, ignites the propellant.

Proof By law, all guns must be nitro-proof tested and stamped accordingly before they can be sold or offered for sale. This means that the assembled action and barrels have been tested to ensure they can withstand a pressure well in excess of that experienced in normal usage. Modern guns are proved for Nitro (smokeless) powder, but many guns still in circulation have only been Black Powder proved. Never use modern cartridges in such a gun: get professional advice if in doubt.

Pump Gun Another form of single-barrelled, repeating shotgun with a magazine in a tube under the barrel. Loading and ejection are achieved by pulling back the sliding fore-end. Pump guns, or pump-action shotguns, are awkward to handle. See Chapter Nine for the legal implications. These guns should not be used for gameshooting but are useful for vermin and pest control.

Punt Gun A large bore gun, almost a small artillery piece, mounted in a punt and used for wildfowling. Such is the recoil that punt guns are usually fired remotely by lanyard (a cord attached to the trigger).

Recoil The force with which a gun moves rearwards into the shoulder when fired. Although superfluous if the gun is held correctly, recoil pads are available to help absorb some of the recoil.

Rifle A firearm with a spirally grooved barrel used for long-range shooting demanding precise accuracy, which fires high velocity ammunition/bullets. Used for shooting any game of the size of deer or greater, rabbits and other small vermin.

Right and Left – vice versa, but usually this way, since that is the sequence the majority of guns are designed to fire in. The definition is: when one bird is killed with the right barrel and another with the left, without reloading or dismounting the gun in between shots.

Rough Shooting Speculative shooting at game in season (or vermin throughout the year) and relying on natural stock. Utterly informal, rough shooting can provide the most enjoyable shooting of all.

Runner Quarry which is wounded and moves away from where it landed or was shot. Runners should not be left without making a determined effort to recover them, unless there are pickers-up nearby who should accordingly be informed of the suspected whereabouts of the runners.

Safety Catch Something of a misnomer since it is a mechanical device which can fail to work. It must always be at safe except when aiming at a target with the intention of shooting at it. There is no other occasion when it should be off. Most shotguns have this as a sliding catch immediately to the rear of the top lever, which is thumb operated. On most guns, breaking the gun returns the catch to the safe position automatically. It is not possible to check the position of the safety catch too often.

APPENDIX

Shoooting School A place that wise gameshots try to visit before the start of the season each year. A short list appears at the end of this book.

Shooting Stick A stick with a handle which tips or opens to form a rudimentary seat and has a guard at the base to prevent it sinking into the ground. Something of an aid to infirmity, it is yet another item to be carried and is very rarely likely to be an essential. Can be useful when awaiting a duck flight.

Shotgun A smooth-bore gun used for shooting game and vermin at relatively short ranges, typically 20–40 yards. The most common size is the 12 bore.

Side-Lock (Hammerless) A refined version of the hammer gun lock and much more expensive. Unlike the normal, squared-off box-lock, it has an elegant rounded plate which lends itself to intricate engraving. Some game shots hold that a side-lock will last longer than a box-lock. Side-locks are easier to detach and some guns are designed with purpose-built detachable locks to facilitate repair, cleaning and maintenance.

Side-by-Side A shotgun with two barrels sitting side-by-side and, in Great Britain, the standard game shooting weapon.

Stand-Peg The place where a Gun stands during a drive. On smarter shoots, each peg will be marked by a stake with a number on the top. Once placed, Guns should indicate their presence to their flanking or neighbouring Guns and never leave the vicinity of their peg unless specifically instructed to do so (usually by their host), until the end of the drive.

Stock The rearmost piece of wood of a shotgun which fits into the shooter's shoulder. Most usually made of walnut, it is easily broken and very expensive to repair. Ideally it should be fitted to the owner for length, cast and bend since, apart from innate inaccuracy on the part of the firer, this is the single biggest cause of missing the target. Stocks can be altered for length relatively easily and inexpensively.

Stop A stop can be a beater or Gun placed to deter game from escaping along the ground any other way except over the Guns.

Striker Correct technical term for firing pin.

Top Lever The conventional mechanism for breaking open a shotgun, situated forward of the safety catch.

Various That part of the bag which is not officially classed as game. Most game books have a 'Various' column.

Vermin Pests and predators that cause considerable damage to crops and game.

Wadding The card and fibre plugs or plastic moulding in a cartridge between the pellets and the propellant which prevents gas from escaping past the pellets when the gun is fired and acts as a piston behind the shot charge.

Walking Gun Usually a Gun who takes his turn to walk with the beaters to shoot birds flying back or out to a side.

Walking-up In which Guns, by walking across a piece of land, flush game before them and shoot. Most game is shot to the front. Beaters may also be interspersed with walking Guns.

Wildfowling The pursuit of wildfowl in wild places usually on the foreshore; principal quarry in Great Britain being: mallard, wigeon, teal and goose.

Note: Barbour, Gore-tex, Hunter and Huskey are all registered trademarks.

APPENDIX 2:
USEFUL ADDRESSES

Voluntary Associations

1. British Association for Shooting and Conservation (BASC), Marford Mill, Chester Rd, Rossett, Wrexham, Clwyd LL12 0HL
Tel.: 0244 570881

Membership is highly recommended and is cheap. Also provides 3rd Pty. liability insurance of £2m. Advice and courses on all shooting aspects, dogs, etc. Quarterly magazine.

2. The British Field Sports Society, 59 Kennington Rd., London SE1 7PZ
Tel.: 071 928 4742

BFSS is a national organization covering all field sports and committed to ensuring their continuance.

3. Country Landowners Association, 16 Belgrave Sq, London SW1X 8PQ
Tel.: 071 235 0511

CLA represents owners of rural & agricultural land. Advises on all land matters, notably legal and taxation. Organizes the Game Fair.

4. The Game Conservancy Fordingbridge, Hants
Tel.: 0425 52381

Possibly the definitive institute, researching practically every aspect of game research and management as well as building and managing a shoot and courses for keepers.

5. National Gundog Association
Tel: 0530 223570

Advice on reputable gundog breeders.

6. British Deer Society, Church Farm, Lower Basildon Berks RG8 9NH
Tel.: 07357 4094

Deer Management.

7. St Hubert Club of Gt Britain, Apes Hall, Littleport, Cambridge.
Tel.: 0353 861090

Deer management and related matters in UK.

8. Scottish Landowners Federation, 18 Abercromby Place, Edinburgh EH3 6TY
Tel.: 031 556 4466

Similar charter to CLA, representing Scottish landowners' interests.

Sporting Publications

1. Shooting Times and Country Magazine – weekly

2. Countrysport Magazine – monthly

3. Country Life Magazine – weekly

4. The Field Magazine – monthly plus summer and Christmas issues

124

Shooting Schools

The few shooting schools mentioned here are the most prominent ones known to the author, spread throughout England, Scotland and Wales. There are many others with equal qualifications, the addresses of which will be available in the Yellow Pages.

1. Holland and Holland Shooting School	Ducks Hill Rd, Northwood, London Tel.: 092 74 25439
2. West London Shooting Grounds	West End, Northolt Tel.: 081 845 1377
3. Apsley Shooting Grounds	Apsley Estate, Andover, Hants Tel.: 0264 62403
4. Humberside Shooting School	Catwick Lane, Brandesburton, Beverley, North Humberside Tel.: 0482 445284
5. Dicksons Colzium Shooting School	Bookings: John Dickson and Son, 21 Frederick St., Edinburgh Tel.: 031 225 4218
7. North Wales Shooting School	Manor Farm, Sealand, Deeside Tel.: 0244 812219
8. Jackie Stewart Shooting School	Gleneagles Hotel, Auchterarder, Stirling, Perthshire, Scotland 07646 3163
9. West Midland Shooting Ground	Hodnet, Shropshire 093924 644
10. Mid Norfolk Shooting School	Deighton Hills Taverham Norwich, Norfolk 0603 860436

INDEX